Points to Ponder
An Exhortation of Scripture

Volume 1, Sermons 1-9

Points to Ponder: An Exhortation of Scripture Sermons of Pastor Bob Joyce

Volume 1, Sermons 1-9

Produced by Willena Joyce
Edited by Katie Wilson and Sabrina McDonald

Table of Contents

Introduction

Bob Joyce is pastor of Household of Faith church in Benton, Arkansas. His sermons and songs have been heard on the Internet for nine years and reach people all over the world. From Europe to South Africa, Pastor Bob reaches people of all situations of faith. Some are lost and come home like the prodigal son. Others are great men of faith who use the sermons to teach tribes and people groups thirsty for the Living Water of God's word.

Now, Pastor Bob's sermons are available in book form. This first volume contains nine sermons, which have been edited for publishing. The small size of the book allows you to take these sermons anywhere, even when Internet is not available, or to be purchased as a gift.

Pastor Bob's sermons are spoken with a warm colloquial style that give the listener a sense of welcome friendship. But even though Pastor Bob's deliver is easy to understand, the ideas discussed within each sermon are profound.

Each message is a balance between the mysterious work of God through the Holy Ghost and the amazing grace and mercy of God to His people. Pastor Bob's theological content rivals the great Bible teachers of history.

The pastor was in grade school when he felt God calling him to preach. He gave his first sermon at the tender age of 12 and has followed that call ever since.

Now people all over the world listen to his sermons each Sunday. Some gather around the computer in a small group. Others fly all the way to Benton, Arkansas, to experience the church first-hand.

Those same sermons can now be enjoyed by readers. Whether under the shade of a tree on a warm spring day or cuddled up next to the fireplace in winter, Pastor Bob's book of sermons is a welcome companion to your spiritual growth.

These sermons were never meant to take the place of your personal Bible study. Bible references have been added to the sermons so you can read them as a companion to the Biblical text. Use these sermons to help you understand the teachings of the New Testament and to challenge your heart and mind in Christ.

However you choose to enjoy Pastor Bob's sermons, keep Jesus the center of your heart and mind, and you will be blessed!

Chapter 1

How to Draw Close to Jesus

I've been thinking lately about the life we have in the Lord. Everyone in this world lives his life as he sees fit to find happiness wherever he can. Most everyone finds an activity they like to do or places they like to go, yet for the most part, people ultimately find life full of heartaches and troubles. Even the good things often turn out to be bad.

Life is full of disappointment for everyone in the world, but the life God gives us in Christ is another type of life. We Christians find that regardless of life's problems we don't have the kind of troubles and problems we knew before.

Still in all, we find we suffer troubles and problems like everyone else. But God gives us hope and peace through it all so our lives are stable. God anchors our souls to that everlasting Rock. Because of that, we're not just floundering on life's sea, but we find refuge in the Lord.

There we found a joy and happiness in the Lord that can't be found anywhere else. Even though there is a certain pleasure and happiness in this world, there is not pleasure and happiness like there is in the Lord. Too many people think they have happiness, but whatever it is that brings that feeling turns around to bite them. And it devours and destroys.

Many people's lives have been destroyed by the indulgence they pursue. But Jesus says, "The [enemy] does not come except to steal, and to kill, and to destroy. I have come that they may have life, and that they may have it more abundantly" (John 10:10). So, there are no regrets in knowing the Lord—no regrets.

Men in the world who have never known the Lord, Jesus's words don't mean anything to them. Life is just life, and they go along doing what they want to do. They think they're content in what they're doing. They think they're happy where they are. But that's because anyone who doesn't know the Lord doesn't know better. They've never experienced God or tasted His presence. They're happy where they are, and they want to be left alone to go along their own way, not knowing what they're missing.

God wants to know the hearts of men, so He intervenes and comes into their lives to bring this new life in Christ. What a difference it makes! Man has found something that he will never let go of. Jesus said the kingdom of God is like a man finding a treasure hidden in a field and with joy he goes and sells all that he has and buys that field, so that he could have that treasure (Matthew 13:44). It was worth so much, so costly and valuable, that the man realized he must have it even if it meant selling everything he had to get it.

That's the way it is with the Lord. When we find Him, we realize He's worth everything. He's worth our lives; He's worth all we have. We're willing to purchase this treasure no matter the sacrifice.

By God's grace, Jesus paid it all. The treasure has already been bought and paid for. All He asks of man is that we say "yes" to Him and "no" to this world—no to the life we knew before and yes to the new life that lies before us.

The old life is full of headache. If you go out and get drunk, what happens? The next morning you wake up with a hangover. Sometimes it's so bad, you wish you could die! Those who pursue drinking for happiness, the indulgence turns around and devours them. That's just one example of thousands. There's nothing in this world that is lasting. Nothing is permanent, and none of it really addresses the thirst and the hunger of the soul.

So, what brings ultimate happiness? The Lord shows us that He is the answer. He is the bread of life, the living water who satisfies completely. And once you've tasted of the Lord and drank of Him then you find it's the path you want to follow—the way He leads you. I don't know what I would do in my life without the Lord. I've known Him all my life and to be without Him … I can't even imagine.

I know what it's like to go out in the world and dabble around a little bit. I tell you, there is nothing worth dabbling around in. I found out that no matter how far you go or what you experiment with, the

Lord's not going to let you go. He's got ahold of you. Aren't you glad the Lord has ahold of you? We all want to wander off from time to time and see what the world has to offer. The Lord gives you a little slack, but He's got you hooked. When He sees you're in trouble He reels you in. Thank God He won't let go.

Man tends to follow after what he thinks is best. But when you find the Lord, you don't want to go down those paths—back to the old life you lived before. You want to walk in the newness of life in the Lord.

Christ makes the difference. Paul says in 2 Corinthians 3:2, "You are our epistle written in our hearts, known and read by all men." In other words, your very life is our testimony. The very life that you live in Christ is our doctrine and our message. How you live and behave before the world is a declaration of truth—talking the talk and walking the walk. And that's what Paul is talking about, essentially saying, everything we preach and teach about the doctrine and gospel of Christ is seen in you.

Did you know you are the living epistle of Christ? What Christ has to say to the world, He's saying it through you and me, through our lives. When you look at your life, what is the Lord saying to the world? How is your conduct in front of others teaching them about the faith?

We often plead, "If only God would speak from heaven!" But God is speaking every day, and He speaks through me and you. Do you see that? He's no longer coming down upon the mountain top shaking the mountain with His mighty power and presence, burning with fire, but He's come to dwell in us. Christ didn't write a book before He left the world, but He did write His words in our hearts. When we speak, we speak His words. Everything that He would want of us would be declared through us.

Therefore, the closer we draw to Him, the more we are filled with Him and declare Him, and the more we see God work through us. Don't you want the Lord to do great works through you? If you do, I'm going to tell you the secret. Ask Him in prayer to draw you closer to Him and be filled with His words and His spirit.

Let your mind be filled with the thoughts of God's word and let them dwell in you constantly. Jesus said, if my words abide in you (and that word "abide" means to live in you), and you live in my word, you can ask what you will and it shall be done unto you (John 15:7).

I believe the reason we're not receiving as much as we would from God is because our hearts and minds are not being filled with His word, but rather filled with everything else of this world.

When we fill our hearts and minds with Christ, and He dwells in us, He becomes our thoughts, hearts, minds, and words. Then we can ask whatever we will, and it will be done because, you see, it's abiding in Christ where we begin to understand what *His* will is.

Knowing God's will means we can be confident. We won't be ashamed or confused or afraid to approach God in prayer and ask for what we want. We know what we're asking for is not for selfish desire but for His glory. God can do anything, but God is not a genie in a bottle who pops out and says, "Okay make three wishes." He doesn't give us whatever our hearts lust for. But as we are filled with God's word, the knowledge of His will begins to open up to us.

Do you want to know God's will? Living according to God's will makes you able to be used by God for other people and see God work in your life. I want to see that. I want to see that more and more.

That's what I've been praying for a lot lately. I've prayed that the Lord would be real to me and let me know His will and draw me close, and the Lord is listening. He will speak to our hearts and show us things. He will guide us and lead us, and we will see amazing works that we've never seen before, if we continue in Him.

If you're saved, this is what the Lord says to you—draw nigh to me. He's not talking to the world. He's talking to His people. He says, "Come in and sup with me, and I will sup with you." Have fellowship with Jesus, and He will fellowship with you and reveal to you His heart. Jesus will tell you what's on His mind.

I want to know what's on His mind, don't you? I want to know what's in His heart. I want to know what Jesus has to say to me and what He wants me to know. Because what He wants me to know is *for* me, and what He wants you to know is for *you*. God has something to reveal to each one of us personally. It's not just general knowledge; it's personal knowledge.

God isn't fooled. He knows where each one of us is in Him, and He knows exactly what every heart needs to know and hear. Oh, we need to hear everything that is good! Anything the Lord has to say is good, and I want to hear it, especially what He has to says to me personally.

Jesus is a *personal* savior, not just a general savior. He's a friend. You can sit down with a close friend and talk like no one else. A close friend is someone you can talk to about secrets, personal things you couldn't with anyone else. Jesus is that close personal friend, and He wants to talk with us, share His feelings, His thoughts, His heart, His words.

I tell you, when you spend time alone with the Lord, that makes you one of the happiest persons around and one of the most pleasant. You become one of those people everyone wants to be around. You also become the kind of person that isn't afraid to speak up for Jesus and tell others about Him. When you speak with Him, He sets your heart on fire. You are the living epistle of Christ, written not with ink but with the spirit of the living God.

There's one writer from the first century that I was reading about the other day. He wasn't an apostle. He was a secular person that lived in those times. He said no one ever said Jesus laughed, but it *was* said that Jesus was one of the most pleasant people you could ever meet.

I do think Jesus was that way—a pleasant sort of fellow. He wasn't one of those big mouths who's the life of the party, hugging everybody and slapping everybody on the shoulder. After a while all the laughing and carrying on gets old, and it's time to settle down and just talk.

I believe Jesus was full of joy—joy unspeakable and full of glory! But it was the kind that never got old. He was the kind of person everybody wanted to be around all the time. And I believe He expressed His joy, kindness, goodness, and rejoiced in spirit in a way that wasn't outlandish or over the top.

The Bible says, several times, that Jesus rejoiced in spirit to the Father. So, if we are the words of Christ, we demonstrate Him by having His spirit, the very nature of Christ. Does that mean God is going to take your personality away from you? Will He take away who you are as an individual? No, I don't believe He does that.

You are who you are, but you're not the same old guy you used to be. You look like you did, talk like you did. Your voice sounds the same; you have the same laughter, same humor. You might seem the same to someone else, but now your joy has been changed. Your laughter is different. Your outlook on life is different because now you know Jesus.

In today's world in America, we have celebrities that everyone tries to be like. We all admire actors, singers, politicians, and presidents. But there's no one I'd rather be like and be around than Jesus. Because He's real—He's the real thing.

Everything else that men have in this world is just an outward show. Throughout the years popular people have said, "If you got to really know the real me, it's a whole lot different than the image." Elvis actually said that about himself, as well as others. It's even hard for them to live up to their own image, the one they created.

But Jesus never had put on a show. If anybody ever had a right to boast, He did. If anybody ever had the right to glory about Himself, Jesus did, but He didn't. He was the perfect human being, the perfect man upon this earth, but He didn't brag about Himself. Jesus gave all the glory to the Father.

When you're touched by Christ, involved with Him, when you pursue Him and get to know Him intimately, what a difference it makes. And the difference it makes in us is not a showy outward change; it's the real thing.

I find the more I know Jesus, the bolder I am. But I'm not bold in the sense of the world—exalting myself or being a braggart. Jesus makes you bold for Him. Jesus makes you happy for Him. He makes you want to talk and speak out, not for yourself, but for Him.

Many people want to be heard and liked by everyone. They want to have something to say that people will pay attention to. But when you get to know the Lord you will find you still want to be heard, but it's not for yourself, it's because of Him.

I want your attention for the Lord. I want you to listen to what I have to say, but because of the Lord. I want you to know and watch, not because of myself but because of Jesus in me.

As we abide in Christ more and more, I pray it gets to the point where we don't even see ourselves anymore, but we only see Him. We won't be living for ourselves; we'll be living for Christ, through Him, and by Him because He is the only one that can make a change in us, and it's the genuine change; it's the real thing.

Paul says, you're written by the spirit of God, not in tablets of stone but in fleshly tablets of the heart. Paul says, I can witness to the fact that what we preach is true and real and good and right because I see the results in you. Therefore, Paul is saying, I know what I preach is right because I can see the difference it's made in you.

The evidence is clear that the gospel is true. The wisdom is clear that the anointing and calling of God on us is true and good. Paul knew it wasn't in his own sufficiency, but the effect he had on the church was because of God. The change that Paul saw was a result of the very words of Christ himself that were preached. Paul knew, brother, when we give what God gives to us, the results are clear!

Why is it that many people today are not seeing the results? Preachers and churches are not seeing the results because, as a whole, we're not giving to others what God has given through His word. We're not sharing what God has told us to share. We're only exalting ourselves. We're only doing things by our own strength and power, our own thoughts and words. As we listen to Christ, we need to tune in, abide, and follow. As we die to self and live to God, reckoning ourselves dead to this world and alive to God, then what we have to give is real. What we share and how we act is real. That is a testimony of Christ, and it is effective. It does its work in this earth, and God's will is done.

Lord, I want my life to be *Your* will done. Not my will, Jesus said, but Your will. If I go my own way, the work can't be accomplished. Salvation can't be accomplished. Redemption will not be accomplished. But if I go *your* way then all will be accomplished. Your will be done.

Are we going to go through our lifetimes not seeing what God wants to do, not seeing all He wants to accomplish in our lives? None of us know what tomorrow may bring, do we? We don't know what next week or next year is going to bring.

But if we stay fastened upon the Lord, fill our lives with Him, and follow Him, then He will show us great and mighty things—all that's joyful, happy, and good.

Live day by day in Christ and see what God will do. See what God unfolds in your life. If we don't seek Him, then we're going to miss out on all the wonderful things God has promised. I'm not saying anyone's salvation will be lost, but I am saying there are so many things that we're going to miss out on when we're not minding the business of God.

What does God want of you and me? What does God want of the church? I believe, first and foremost, God wants everyone of us to be absolutely joyful, content, and at peaceful rest in Him. God wants every one of us to be totally filled and satisfied in Him. And so this anointing that we have which is the Holy Ghost that God gives to us, John tells us that He teaches us all things. So, we should walk in that knowledge.

Every day, as we walk in Christ, God is being glorified in us. Isn't that wonderful? It's wonderful to know that we're not just dead wood floating along. We're not just old dead stumps on a log, as the preachers used to say. But we're living and giving glory to God.

Lord, how can I give you glory today? I believe the Lord would reply and say, "Walk close to me, draw near to me, and I will show you things to come. I will show you and teach you, and you will know."

It reminds me of the story of the prodigal son in Luke 15:11-32. Do you remember what happened when the prodigal son came home? The father welcomed him back into his house. The father embraced him, gave him new clothes, shoes, and rings on his fingers. His father gave him everything he needed to live, the best that he had. The father even killed the fatted calf to have a feast in his lost son's honor.

I'm sure the son realized that his father gave him a second chance at life. He gave him an opportunity to live. Maybe he thought, "I was dead but now I'm alive because my father has welcomed me back into his home and his life." Now his life will be good and productive when it could have been ruined.

Jesus told this story and He said the family had music and danced and made merry. They rejoiced! The Bible doesn't say this, but surely that prodigal son, after rejoicing and dancing and thinking about what all that had happened to him, maybe he sat in the corner thinking to himself, "Oh I'm really happy, but I don't deserve how happy I am. I've been bad … terrible! I've been the worst. I don't have a right to show my happiness. If I dance and rejoice people will look down their noses at me and think, "What are you doing there dancing? You know what you did. You know how you lived. You ought to sit down and be quiet."

The truth is, the prodigal son *didn't* have the right to rejoice on his own merit. Do you know what gave him the right? His father. The father welcomed him back into the fold of the family, embracing him. That's what gave him the right and confidence to show how thankful and happy he was. He knew he would never ever go back out in the world again. He was in his father's house to stay.

There was someone who did look down on the prodigal son. It was his older brother that made the complaint. He told his father, "I've been with you all this time and haven't gone out in the world, and you never did this for me. Now here my brother comes, after wasting all of

15

your money on riotous living, and you throw him a party. Yet, I have never let you down."

Let me tell you, there's always somebody who thinks you shouldn't make such a display of worship and thanksgiving. They'll say, "You're supposed to be quiet here." But the goodness, mercy, and love of God gives us the right and the privilege to demonstrate our thankfulness and praise to Him for what He's done for us.

Don't let anybody ever tell you that you don't have a right to praise God. You have every right. Don't let anybody ever tell you that you should never get excited. You act like that because of what God's done for you, and He gives you every confidence because you know what He's done for you. If it's good enough for the Father, it's good enough for me. If it's okay with my Father for me to cut a rug a little bit and do a little jig, I'm going to dance a little jig because it's okay with Him. *He* brought me home. *He* welcomed me back. What Christ has done for us gives us the right, opportunity, and confidence to proclaim His goodness and to show the world what God has done for you.

Be that written epistle; *be* that joy of the Lord demonstrated. Show the peace of God and the love of God. Show the love that God has had for you. Show the goodness and mercy that God has shown to you.

Jesus said, your father in heaven is merciful to the good and to the evil, to the just and the unjust. And that gives us a right to celebrate! That gives us all the confidence we need because He has embraced us and brought us in and made us His own.

So, I don't live to satisfy others. I'm not living and preaching to please man but the One who called me, the One who embraced me, the One who welcomed me home. He made me a member of His family, and He gives me the right.

That's why I want to get close to the Lord because in myself, I'm a mess. Without Him, I'm nothing but a failure. In myself I can't do anything right. The only good thing that ever happened to me was Jesus, and through Him, everything else is good.

The devil will beat you down, slap you in the face. People will beat you down. The things you think you want and like and pursue will beat you down and try to destroy you. Only the Lord lifts you up. He cleans you up, takes off all those dirty clothes, washes you, and clothes you with a robe of righteousness. He pours oil over you and fills you with wine. He comforts and cares for you. He loves you and meets all your needs in order to make you a son of His household. He makes your life brand new.

Only God can do that. And who wouldn't want it?

Now that God has done all of these great things for us, are we going to sit around His house and say, "Boy, this chair sure is comfortable, Father. It's a whole lot better than that pig pin out there." The Lord will say, "I want you to get up off that chair and go out there and do some work for me today. There's work to be done! I didn't call you just to sit in the house all day. I called you to go out into the fields and go forth in my name. I called you to be my living epistle, to be my light in this world."

And what did Jesus do when He was here? Did He sit around on the couch all day, eating potatoes chips and hot dogs? No! Brother, He was out there in the highways and hedges, talking to people. His was a light to the world. And now we must be a light because He is the light in us.

Lord, shine in me! Lord, I want to be nearer and closer. I want to be filled with you. Draw me nearer. Oh Lord, let me know you even more. Lead me where you want me to go. Help me do whatever you want of me. My life is yours. All that I have is yours—all the money in my pocket, the house where I live, my family—everything that is nearest and dearest to me is yours. Do with me what you will. Forgive me for failing you. Forgive me, Father, for going my own way. Lead me and guide me. Lord, I want to hear your voice and know you more and more. Because you're worth it. You're the real thing. In Jesus' name, Amen.

Chapter 2

At the Feet of Jesus

I wanted to briefly touch upon a certain woman I was reading about in the Bible, Mary, the sister of Lazarus. There were two sisters, Martha and Mary, and Lazarus, their brother. As I was reading the scripture, I found that this Mary was mentioned three times, and in each instance, you find her at the feet of Jesus. That struck me. I believe Mary had one of the greatest and most precious testimonies of anyone because each time we find Mary sitting or kneeling at the feet of Jesus.

The first time we see Mary at Jesus' feet was when Jesus went to visit them in their home in Bethany (Luke 10:48-42). I'm sure Lazarus was there. This was before Lazarus died. I'm sure everyone was sitting around in that house eager to hear what Jesus had to say. (I know I would have been!) Mary was one of those eager listeners, too.

Martha, her sister, was busy in the kitchen preparing the meal for everybody. And she began to be a little bit perturbed because no one was helping her. There must have been a lot of people there, and she had a lot of serving to do. It was quite a lot, all those people and getting their dishes ready and food put out. You know what it's like, making sure everybody has something to eat and drink, and see to it that everybody is served. Martha began to be troubled about that, and kind of upset.

So, Martha went to Jesus and said, "Lord don't you care that I have to do this by myself? Will you please bid Mary to come and help me?" (vs. 40). But Jesus looked at her and said, "Martha, Martha, you are careful and troubled about many things, but there's one thing that you lack that you need, and Mary has chosen that good part, and it shall not be taken away from her" (vs. 41-42).

The Bible says Jesus loved Martha and her sister and Lazarus. He loved Martha as much as He loved Mary, but Martha was troubled saying, "We've got to get this done. We've got to make sure everybody gets enough to eat and drink." There's a great lesson right there for every one of us. We have become troubled about so many things in life that we think are so important. But Jesus didn't seem to think that was quite as important.

Can you imagine what was going through Martha's mind? How many times have you been caught up in life, and all kinds of thoughts go through your mind—questions, doubts, grumbling, complaints? You get fed up, tired, discouraged. You get worried or frustrated, and it's all because "this has got to be done; this is necessary." All it does is make you unhappy.

How many times have I found myself caught up in the moment frustrated, aggravated, worried, upset, and wondering, "What am I going to do?" I'll say, "Lord, will you please send somebody over here to help me? I don't know what I'm going to do here. This is important!"

And all the time the Lord is saying, "Stop what you're doing. This is not so important. You're too concerned about too many things. You're worrying about too much. Stop what you're doing."

Mary chose to come lay at Jesus' feet and listen to what He said, and when she was criticized, the Lord said, "I'm not going to take that away from her. I'm not going to tell her go in there and help you."

I'm sure that compounded the frustration for Martha. You know, when one thing begins to aggravate you, other things make it worse.

19

Sometimes I can get aggravated at my wife, or she can get aggravated at me. Usually, I'm not really angry with her. Something else is troubling me. Something's been on my mind, bothering me all day, and I take it out on her. That's what was wrong with Martha.

Jesus ended up pointing out Martha's heart. But what does Martha need to do? She needs to get in there and say, "Hey folks, if you want anything to eat come and get it. I'm going to come in here and sit at Jesus' feet with Mary, and I'm going to listen."

That works for me every time. When I get troubled and frustrated over things in life, what do I do? I go straight to God's word, open it up, and begin to read what Jesus says. Instantly my mind is at ease. He calms the storm that's raging in my mind and heart. And Jesus' words bring peace.

And you know what? He's not going to take that away. Things in this life are designed by the enemy to take away our peace. But when Jesus gives us peace, nothing can take it away.

The Lord Himself is not going to tell you to get out of His presence. He isn't going to say, "I haven't got time for you." He's going to say, "Come on in here and sit right down with me and let's talk awhile." It's exactly what you needed.

A lot of times, if you have a friend in this world that you can call him up on the telephone. Sometimes I call my good friend Leon. Just having the company of a good friend for a little while helps a lot. It kind of makes you forget about all your own problems. And after hearing their problems, you might say, "Boy, I thought I had problems, but they make me feel good." Then you pray for them, and maybe that's what you both needed.

That's the love of Jesus, and that's the love that He has for all of us. The heart of the Lord is pure love. And this is what Mary found out for herself. She found an intimate spiritual relationship in her heart with the Lord. She made a connection with Jesus.

When Martha was busy, encumbered with serving and cooking and all this, she wasn't making connection; she wasn't hearing. Jesus loved her, but Martha was too busy to find anything out about His love. She was too busy to find that intimate relationship with Him that Mary was finding. But Mary found it!

In the days of Jesus, women were not allowed to do much. They were separated in the synagogue from the men. They weren't allowed to speak. But Jesus kind of changed all that. Jesus made women important in society. Jesus gave women an equal place.

So, here's Mary sitting with all the men crowding around. Imagine Jesus sitting in the middle, maybe up against the wall, and everybody is gathered around Him, crowding in, sitting on the floor or wherever they can. These men came in there, and here's this one girl.

She walks in with her head low, meek, and lowly. She gets right in front of Jesus, sits down at His feet, and looks up in His eyes and says, "I want to hear what He has to say." She fastened her eyes and heart upon the Lord. She didn't care what was going on around her. It didn't bother her that her sister was so troubled with all the serving. She wasn't concerned about anything except being with Jesus.

And Jesus said she had chosen the good part that's not going to be taken away from her. He wasn't going to bid her to do anything else. He wanted her to sit right where she was and listen to what He was saying.

Later on, we read that Lazarus died (John 11:1-44), and before Jesus got into town, the Bible says Martha ran out to meet Him. Martha said, "Lord, if you'd been here my brother would not have died, but I know now that whatever you ask God He'll give it to you." And we know the story. Jesus said, "Your brother shall rise again."

Martha said, "I know he'll rise again in the resurrection on the last day." And Jesus said, "I am the resurrection and the life. He that believes on me though he were dead, yet shall he live. He that lives and believes on me shall never die, do you believe this?" She said, "Yes, Lord, I believe you are the Christ the son of God that came into the world" (vs. 25-27). Martha ran back to tell her sister, "The Master calls for you."

Mary was still in the house. She didn't go out with Martha the first time. She stayed behind, weeping and crying. And her neighbors and friends were gathered around, and they were with her weeping and comforting her. She was just heartbroken.

But when Martha came and told her the Master calls for you, she got up immediately and ran out the door. All the mourners said, "She's going out to the grave to weep. Let's go with her." But Mary ran to meet Jesus.

Then there was something Mary did that Martha didn't do. As soon as she came to where Jesus was, she fell down at His feet crying. That seems to be Mary's place throughout the scripture. She's always found at the feet of Jesus. She says while weeping, "Lord if you'd been here my brother would not have died."

At that point Jesus was troubled in His spirit. He groaned, and Jesus wept. Everybody was weeping; everybody was crying. But Mary knew her place. It wasn't standing up in front of Him or standing off to the side and looking on. She fell at His feet.

Why did Mary do that? Martha didn't do that. The others didn't do that. But Mary, again, fell at His feet. I believe something happened in the heart of Mary the first time she fell at Jesus' feet. A special love and respect for Jesus began to develop. She realized, maybe more than anyone, who Jesus was and what He was. She knew He wasn't just a man, just a friend or miracle worker. She knew He is the Lord. He's not just the son of Mary and Joseph, He's the Son of God. She knew if Jesus is Lord, then I'm His, and He is mine. If He is the Lord, I am His servant. If He is the Lord, then He is the one that I look to and bow down before.

Some of us say, "Jesus is my Lord." But I want to ask you these questions: Is He the Lord of your life? Do you honor Him? Do you respect Him? Does He have your attention? Have you listened to Him? Do you know His heart? Do you know what He says to you? Do you know His love for you?

I believe Mary knew His love for her. I believe when we see Jesus and enter in with Him in that glorious place called Heaven, we're going to fall down at His feet, just like Mary.

John saw the Lord in revelations, and he saw His eyes in a flame of fire. John saw His hair white like wool, His feet as brass burned in an oven. And Jesus glistened like the sun. John said, "When I saw Him, I fell at His feet as one that was dead" (Revelation 1:17). Why? Because Jesus is the Lord, and John is His servant. Mary knew this.

What a testimony Mary had; what a heart she had. Every one of us needs to give place to the Lord in our lives. Give Him the honor and respect that is due Him and bow before Him and kiss His feet.

Don't exalt yourself above the Lord. Don't boast yourself against Him. Don't you know that God could just take one little bitty finger, push you over, and that would be the end of you? He can do that, but He doesn't.

You see, God's not like us. That's not even in His mind. That's not in His heart. He doesn't want to rub you out. He doesn't want to talk mean to you. He's not angry with you. You may be caught up in all kinds of problems. There may be something carrying you away. You may think God doesn't love you or care about you at all.

But I've got news, good news for you. He does care about you!

The Lord's been checking my heart lately. He says, "Son, at the center of my message in my word is my love for you. The very heart of the gospel is my love for you and the whole world." God's not angry. There's one scripture in the Old Testament that says, "For the mountains shall depart, and the hills be removed; but my kindness shall not depart from thee, neither shall the covenant of my peace be removed, saith the Lord that hath mercy on thee" (Isaiah 54:10).

Oh, what a great God! What a great and mighty God we serve. We haven't yet understood His great love. He not only loves us, but He also wants us to find out more about His love. He wants us to get in there and kneel at His feet and hear what He has to say, so that we'll know His love for us.

Talk about making you walk right and talk right … His love will do that. God loves you no matter what you do. He'll teach you and show you what to do and what not to do. But what changes you is knowing His love. It will lead you, guide you, and strengthen you. You'll come to know Him, and every time you see Him, you'll want to fall down at His feet like Mary.

That's where I find peace for my mind. I get troubled about everything else out there in this world. Even in this very room, I can be troubled. Jesus can be in the room, and you can still be troubled about things, just like the disciples. Everybody can be mad at each other—anger, strife, malice.

So, what do you do about it? You do like Mary. Drop the dishes. Forget about the food. Put the bills down on the table. Quit fussing at your husband or wife. And determine in your heart, "I'm going to get at the feet of Jesus. I'm going to find peace with Him. I'm going to look in His heart and hear what He's got to say to me."

If you're like me, you're tired of being caught up in things of this world. I want peace in my life. I'm getting old now, and I want peace. When you're young, you've got all that strength, and you're full of vinegar. You're going to rule the world and tell everybody what to do.

But when you start to calm down and grow up a little bit, you get in there with Jesus. That's when you start to ask, "Jesus, what can I do for you? I want to be your servant. I don't want to be a hard head; I want to be an old softy. How can I love you? I don't want to mistreat you or be angry with you. I don't want to quarrel and argue; I want to love you."

Let's go to Jesus, and then we can learn how to love one another and get along. How about getting there with Mary. Sit down and be quiet, and let's let the Lord fill our hearts with His love.

Who knows … the Lord may just snap His finger and all this food will suddenly appear in everybody's lap. You don't know what He's going to do. Martha, you don't have to serve the food. The Lord will put it out there. Don't be so troubled about it. Sit down and maybe the Lord will put it all together.

That doesn't mean we should all go home and don't serve the company. If company comes to your house, you better serve them. If you come to my house, I'll serve you. I'd ask you if you want something to drink or eat. I'd say, "Sit down and have a seat, relax, take your shoes off, stay awhile." Let's not get so busy about things that it interrupts our love and our fellowship with the Lord. That'll not be taken away.

We find Mary again, a third time.

This time, Jesus went into the house with a certain man to make supper (Matthew 26:6-13). (There sure were a lot of people making supper for the Lord, wasn't there? He didn't have to worry about fixing His dinner. When you're with Jesus you don't have to worry about what you're going to eat next, there's always somebody ready to feed you.) So, He went into the man's house, a man named Simon.

As Jesus was there eating, Mary, this same Mary, came in with a box of very precious ointment in an alabaster box and anointed Jesus' feet. One scripture says she poured it on His head, as well.

She came in, even in the midst of whatever was going on in that moment. Maybe Jesus was sitting at the table eating and fellowshipping with Simon and the disciples. Then suddenly this woman comes in, and she's at His feet again. But this time she's got something very precious and costly.

Mary doesn't hand Jesus the box and say, "Here, Lord, here's a box of oil." She opens it up, and pours the oil on His feet. There she is again—at the feet of Jesus. She's not standing or sitting at the side. She's not sitting at the table with everybody else.

I love Mary. The more I read about Mary, the more I admire the woman. It reminds me of my wife. I believe my wife is the same way in her spirit. She loves the Lord so much she can talk about what the Lord's done for her in her life. She can't tell her testimony without weeping, and she's been saved for over thirty years. Every time she tells the story, no matter where she's at—church, home, on the telephone … she's weeping.

Because she felt so grateful, Mary brought Jesus expensive oil in an expensive box. The alabaster box itself is worth a lot of money. Alabaster is an expensive material, and then the ointment inside was precious, very costly.

So, what is she doing putting that on Jesus' feet like that? Think of the money! That could have been sold and given to the poor folks. People looked at her grumbling and said, "You're wasting it, putting it on His feet."

But Mary didn't care what they thought. She poured it on His feet, washing His feet with her hair. The Bible says in one place, she poured it on His head. She was anointing His body with this ointment. And I don't know what made her do it, but I believe she was pouring out her love.

Like Mary, we say, "Oh Lord, you're worth everything I have. The things I count most precious in my life I give to you because you're the Lord, and I love you. You're worthy. Take my life, take my oil, my money, my family. Take everything I have, Lord. All that I have is yours."

And people look and say, "That's silly. You are a fanatic about Jesus." And I say, "Yes, I am a fanatic about the Lord!" Call me a fanatic if you want, but He's the Lord. He's the Lord of heaven and earth. He is the one who created all things. He is the King of kings. He is the Son of the living God. And He is worthy.

One day *every* knee shall bow. And where are they going to bow? Before His feet. Every man is going to bow, every woman, child, angel, demon. Every creature great and small are going to bow before Him in all of His glory and power. One day the world's going to know when Jesus steps out on the clouds in front of the whole world. They're going to know that all creation is His, and it will bow before its maker, the one who brought all things into existence and holds all things together by the word of His power.

Yes, all will bow before Him. And then the whole world will know that their gods are false. Their religions are lies. And all will know that Jesus Christ is the Savior of the world.

But for now, until that day, my heart is His. I feel His glory and power and love so great inside of me that sometimes it seems I can't contain it.

Have you ever felt His great power and presence so wonderfully that you felt like you could explode inside? God loves us so much. Do you know what He's going to do? One day, He is going to give us a body that will allow us to look into His eyes and behold His face. We'll be able to look upon His glory and enjoy His presence, and we're going to see Him as He is.

Mary anointed Jesus' head and feet. She wiped His feet with the hairs of her head. The onlookers grumbled and complained, but Jesus said leave her alone; do not trouble her. In the same way, the world is telling you, "Don't do that. That's foolish. Don't act that way. That's fanatical." They'll chide you, "Are you one of those crazy people?" And the Lord is telling them, "Leave them alone. What they're doing is a good thing."

Mary anointed Jesus' body for burial. She didn't know that, but Jesus knew that. That means His love for her had already been set in motion. It was set in motion before the world began. God is light and light of love. In Him there is no darkness at all. God's love for us sent Jesus into the world to die on that cross and be buried for us because He loved us.

This intimate relationship, this love that Mary was feeling with the Lord, was that same love He was sharing. She didn't understand that love. She didn't know what that love meant or what the love was going to do for her. She didn't know what that love could accomplish in her life. But Mary loved the Lord and knew His love.

When Jesus said Mary was preparing Him for burial, He was already proclaiming victory. He was saying, "I'll lay down my life for her and for you. My life is your life. My love is your love. All that I have, Mary, is yours and all that you have is mine. What you do for me now is good. You may not know everything that you're doing but I see what you're doing. You may not understand why you do the things you do, but you're willing to give all."

That's the love of God. Anytime you feel that you want to give all to the Lord, that's the love of God working in your heart. When you look into His eyes, hear His words, and you want to bow before Him at His feet, then that love is returned back to you.

Isn't that wonderful? It's like the relationship between a husband and wife, if you really love one another. I say to my wife, "Honey, all that I have is yours, what little there is." And she says the same: "All I have belongs to you. I give all that I have, all the most valuable things in my life."

That's love, the binding force. It holds the relationship together. Love is the bond. The Bible calls it charity, the bond of perfection. It's what makes us one and influences how we think, feel, and act. It makes us worship God, and He loves us right back. He's pouring out to us, and we're pouring back to Him. He's giving to us, and we're giving it right back to Him.

This is what God wants. It delights the Lord. This is what Mary was doing. And Jesus was really saying, "I lay down my life; I give my body for you."

And Jesus does that for me, even though, left to myself, I want to be troubled about life. I want to sit around with everybody else and talk about Jesus, but never really take His love to heart. But, like Mary, when I get down at His feet and humble myself, I can say, "Lord, I love you because I know your love for me, and I want to honor you with my life."

I want to honor the Lord at the grocery store, driving down the street, singing in the church and at home. Lord, I want to honor you with my time, my everything.

But sometimes we don't honor God. And He loves us anyway. It happens to me sometimes. And then I pray, "I don't want to fail you, Lord. I don't want to forsake you. I don't want to forget you, God. If I do, please forgive me and bring me back. I know your love will always embrace me even when I turn you away."

Sometimes we may not understand why we should pour out all we have like Mary. We don't see any purpose or reason for doing it. But we do it anyway because we love Him, and one day we're going to find out the reason why.

Chapter 3

What is Prophecy?

I want to speak to you a little bit about prophecy and what it is. This is what the Lord laid on my heart to share with you. In Revelation 19:9-10, John has seen an angel. Read with me, "Blessed are they which are called unto the marriage supper of the Lamb. And he saith unto me, These are the true sayings of God. And I fell at His feet to worship Him. And He saith unto me, See thou do it not: I am thy fellowservant, and of thy brethren that have the testimony of Jesus: worship God: for the testimony of Jesus is the spirit of prophecy."

Every one of us usually thinks of prophecy as future events that will come to pass. Isn't that true? But the Lord laid something on my heart about prophecy that I've never really conceived. When I read the end of this verse, that's when the light came on. It's very simple when we think about it all from cover to cover in the Bible from Genesis to Revelations.

First, let me back up and say this. There are two kinds of people in this world. The one that lives out their lifetime pursuing whatever it is they want to do in life. That can be a rich man, a poor man, and everyone in between. But this type of person simply lives life without care. He's born, grows up, and lives in this world paying no mind to anything but his own desires. Some of them make great achievements, pursue goals, and reach those goals. Some don't. They believe we're all just common everyday ordinary people who live and die.

But they don't have God at the center of their lives, and they don't really know what they've missed. So, God becomes less. He's not important to them at all. And it's equally not important to understand eternity, judgement, and what's to come after you die. These people don't even give it a thought. They think we all just live out our lives and die and that's the end of it. That's one group.

The second kind of people are those living with Christ in the very center of their lives. They live according to the dictates of God. It doesn't matter what kind of work they do or what life consists of, the main goal of their lives is to follow the Lord. He is all important to their lives. They look for His direction and His will. They look for what it is He wants for them to fulfill and accomplish.

But this life is not the end of it; it's only the beginning. This group thinks about all these things. We think about life, death, the judgement, and all other future events that are coming. It's always in the back of our minds, and sometimes in the forefront.

So, the whole concept of life in Christ is all important and absolutely necessary for us to live. We couldn't live without it. Because once you've tasted of the Lord and come to the Lord for yourself, He becomes the most important one in your whole life. He's more important than money, family, or your house. He's more important than anything you want to accomplish or pursue. Even the Apostle Paul, who was a mighty man in wisdom, said about himself, "All I've ever learned, all that I know compared to Christ is nothing."

So, the one group says self is all important. The other group says God is all important. Now that I've said that, let's get to prophecy.

What does my life in Christ and yours have to do with prophecy? Let me tell you—everything! Everything has to do with prophecy. What do I mean by that? Let me explain.

From Genesis to Revelation, everyone who has ever spoken by the word and spirit of God, all the words of God spoken for edification, comfort, warning, salvation, deliverance, obedience, growth, anything spoken for our good in Jesus' name, it all points to one Person.

For those of us who are saved, our lives center around *one* person, Jesus Christ. Therefore, the words that we speak point and come from Him. He is not only the *object* of our words; He is the *source* of our words. When we speak of Christ, we're not only speaking *of* Him but *from* Him.

The words that we have, the ones we know came from God, what do they say to us? If I come to another brother in the Lord and encourage him because he needs it, what am I doing? What is it in me that's speaking to you? The source is exactly what John said here in Revelation—the testimony of Jesus is the spirit of prophecy.

How do we live, from moment to moment, day to day? When we speak words of Christ to one another, it's for the *now*, right now. If you need a word of encouragement because you're down, the Lord sends somebody to encourage you at that moment.

And the lasting effect is not only for that moment but also for that moment forward. Everything in your life is always moving forward in Christ. It doesn't remain stagnant. Jesus is the Great I *Am*. Not the great I *was* or *used to be* but the Great I *Am*. Jesus said in Revelation, "I am He that liveth and was dead, and behold I'm alive forevermore" (Revelation 1:18). He also said to the people in the garden who went to arrest Him, "I Am" (Matthew 26:36-56). He spoke to the Jews in the temple and He said, "Before Abraham was, I Am" (John 8:58).

God is the forever *now*. He is the source of all things. He never had a beginning. The Father always was, always is, and always will be. We can't comprehend that. You and I as creatures of God can only comprehend the idea that we had a beginning, and in Christ Jesus, there will be no ending.

So, everything you have in your heart and spirit that comes out of your mouth inspired by Christ, that's prophetic. Those words that God intends for you is His prophecy for you.

Everyone wants to know, what is God's will? What are we really talking about? We're asking about the future. We want to know what you do at this moment and into the future. What you do today by the will of God and what you do tomorrow and so on.

God is telling you His will through all these sources—the encouragement and admonition of the brothers and sisters in Christ, the teachings of the preacher, and other sources. And He gives you the interpretation through His word.

When the preacher gets up to preach, what is he doing? He's bringing forth the treasures of Christ. Everything in the Bible testifies of Christ. Every sermon I preach testifies of Christ. Every person that gets saved and born again and serves God has the testimony of Christ. Everything about our lives every day, when we run errands, walk along the street, or go home among family and friends—our whole lives are a testimony to Jesus Christ. You're living out His revelation from moment to moment, and we can see how God works through the testimony of the way we live.

I'm talking about those things that are going to happen in your life as you follow the Lord—as you obey, love, serve, and testify of Him. You will begin to experience moments of admonishment and encouragement.

For example, somebody might stand up and give you what we call a "personal word" and tell you something about your life that you know is true. The person delivering the message is under the inspiration of the spirit of God who brings to their mind a message that deals with you personally, things that only you know about. In that moment, you know God is talking to you. And you understand in your spirit, you're hearing the word coming to you. It is admonishing and encouraging you, prompting you to move forward into what God wants you to do.

So, every word of Christ is a prophetic word. Jesus is speaking, but He is doing the work through someone else. And we know when it comes from the spirit of God because it transforms and transpires in us. It makes a change in us, transforming our lives continually.

God never changes, but we do. So, everything in the word of God that concerns us has to do with our future and our growth. Everything in Christ has to do with our benefit. God wants what's best for us. God doesn't need anything. He doesn't need to change. Everything good comes from God. But God has created us so that we can come to know Him. He wants us to see great things, and the longer we know Him, we see better and clearer all the time.

That's God's will for us, and what He's doing is for our benefit. God is revealing His will for us every day if we'll listen. All we have to do is keep it in our hearts and let it dwell there. His words will transform us. And that's prophetic.

Talk about your future! There are things that God gives a man to prophesy, like in the book of Acts. That book talks about a prophet who told about a great drought, a famine, and it happened just like he said. Every time a man is inspired by the spirit of God to say something, he's got to say it. Whatever he says by the word of the Lord, it will come to pass.

When I get up and preach the word of God, and I'm inspired by the Holy Ghost to say something, I've got to say it! Something is going to happen; it's going to come to pass. Whatever I say, if you listen and receive it and put it into your heart and let it grow there, it'll cause something to happen in your life. That's prophetic.

The spirit of prophecy is the testimony of Jesus. Jesus talked about Himself to His followers in Luke 24. As He was walking along the road to Emmaus after the resurrection, these men were sad. He asked them, "What manner of communications have ye one to another as you walk?" (v. 17). And they told him about what happened with Jesus, not knowing they were talking to Him.

And Jesus said, "Oh fools and slow of heart to believe all that the prophets have spoken. Ought not Christ to have suffered these things and to enter into His glory?" (v. 25-26). He said, "These are the words that I spoke to you, while I was yet with you, that all things must be fulfilled, which was written in the law of Moses, and the prophets, and in the Psalms, concerning me.

"Thus it is written, and it behooved Christ to suffer, and rise from the dead the third day: And that repentance and remission of sins should be preached in His name among all nations, beginning at Jerusalem, and you are witnesses of these things" (v.44-48).

Everything that was said about Jesus was fulfilled in Him. And now, He says, you will be witnesses of these things. That's as prophetic as what happened to Him. Everything that happened to Christ would happen to His disciples from that point forward. Christ was saying, "You are going to be witnesses of this, and I'm going to send the promise of the Father to you."

What's Jesus doing there? He's prophesying. Do you think Jesus Christ is just talking in the air? Do you think Jesus is humming along? No, everything that Jesus said is prophetic. Everything that Jesus said then to the disciples is exactly what's going to happen. He didn't say "maybe" or "well, it might happen." No, He was telling them, it's coming. I want you to go to Jerusalem and wait because it's coming.

Jesus told them, "You're going to testify of me. You're going to testify everywhere you go. I'm going to send you all over the world. You're going to start here at Jerusalem and spread out everywhere. And the whole world is going to know who I am." You talk about prophecy! You can't get any greater than that, can you?

So then, what is that saying to us? It's saying that the Holy Spirit, when He comes, He will give us power. "Ye shall receive power after the Holy Ghost is come upon you and ye shall be witnesses unto me in Jerusalem, Judea, Samaria and unto the uttermost parts of the earth"

(Acts 1:8). The Holy Spirit then comes, and He continues in us and in the Church that prophetic spirit. That spirit constantly unveils, reveals, and guides. It transforms us and makes us new. It causes us to know Jesus and makes us a great witness of everything.

God does a great work in the earth through the spirit of Jesus that's in us. It's always in us. It's constantly in us. Every once in a while, God gives us a particular word to speak to somebody, and that's okay. But it's all the same—the prophetic word of the testimony of Jesus Christ in your life.

Every word that's given to us of encouragement is a testimony of Jesus. Every word that's given to us whether it's preaching, prophesying, speaking in tongues and interpreted, or however it's given, even through song, testimony, or conversation. Every word we give about Jesus Christ—that is the spirit of prophecy! It's all the word of God through His people.

Now listen, Paul says all of you can prophesy. He says some of you want to speak in tongues. He says it's wonderful—speak in tongues. Don't forbid speaking in tongues. But greater is he who prophesies than he who speaks in tongues.

So, if you want to speak in tongues in church, pray that you interpret what you say. If you don't get interpretation, keep your mouth shut. Don't speak. Because, Paul says, it's better that the people hear the interpretation. Those in the church are not getting any benefit from tongues if they don't understand what you're saying. But if they are given understanding, then there's benefit.

Why is that beneficial? Because that's the prophetic spirit of the testimony of Jesus Christ. It gives encouragement. It shows us the way to go, how to act and behave. And what is everything that God requires of us? God wants everything of us right now and from now on, into the future. His prophecy is for today, tomorrow, next week. It's for the rest of your life.

Christ is not only important to us here on Sunday. He's also important when we wake up on Monday morning. It's like the old preacher used to say, this is not just a Sunday religion. It's for Monday, Tuesday, Wednesday, Thursday, Friday—it's for everyday of the week! Because everything about my life is growing—it's going in a future direction.

If you look at a plant, what does it do? It grows. It doesn't go backward. You don't see a plant shrink back down into the ground and become roots. It comes up and grows upward. Everything God made grows upward, away from where it's rooted. And it begins to produce, showing that God made it. That's exactly the way we are in Christ and that's prophetic.

God says let everything grow in the field. Let the trees grow, the grass grow, the flowers grow—everything that I planted. What does that mean? That means everything has a future, a purpose—that's prophetic. God doesn't focus on the past. He focuses on the future.

When we speak of Jesus Christ, we're not speaking of someone dead. We're speaking of somebody who causes the church to grow. He causes every one of us to spring forth and become strong in the Lord.

Somebody might say, "Well, I was strong yesterday, but what about today? I used to know that Lord. I used to be pretty good in the church, and I would shout and dance. But what about now?"

Let me tell you, Christ is not a dead, stagnant pool in the swampy country, like I used to fish in when I was a kid. Jesus Christ is living water that flows constantly. His water is fresh, clean, and pure. His water flows and moves, and it moves the church. That's prophetic. That's talking about *my* future; that's talking about *my* life. If that's not happening in your life, you need to taste of that water and let it bring you life! Read His word and let it bring you life!

There's no end to Jesus Christ. There's a beginning with me, but there's no beginning with Him. He's always been. Jesus said everything the prophets said about me had to be fulfilled. And all the prophets pointed to Him. Every single word.

In the same way, every word inspired by God of every Christian points to Christ. Our testimony of Jesus shows His power. Our witness of Christ shows the power of God in our lives. And the power of God in our lives shows the world how real God is when they see Him through us.

When we are in Christ, we should be growing! God doesn't stunt our growth. He makes us grow. God doesn't call us unto dead; He calls us unto life which lives on and on. The church is not dead. The church is alive! If you're in Christ Jesus, you're made alive. And if you're alive, you're going to grow. If you're alive, you've got a future. It will never die.

Do you ever feel like, "I'm a Christian, but, boy, I just don't feel like I used to. I feel like I'm not getting anywhere." Then you need a prophetic word of the Lord. You need a word of encouragement, something that brings faith to your heart. But you don't really need someone to say it. Just open up your Bible and read it. Hear it with your ears. Hear it with your heart. God is speaking to you a word of faith. The Bible is speaking about your growth, your future, your life, and what you can accomplish.

What does accomplish mean? The word accomplish itself means something that will be completed in the future. And faith is accomplished in Christ. Faith believes what God says. Even though we may not see God's promises with our eyes, we believe them in our hearts. It may not be accomplished yet, but it will be accomplished. Whatever God says will happen, it will happen. God has always proven Himself to be true.

Now, if we preach the word of God, then we stand on the word of God. And we expect to experience all that God promised us. All these promises, like the song goes, nothing compares to the promises we have in Him, and those promises deal with our lives every single day.

Right now, moments are passing. Seconds are ticking away. Another second is in the past now. So, what am I saying? We are living continually in the future. Everything about us is continually moving forward. I'm getting older every moment. And we're either learning or we're not; we're growing or we're not. We're moving forward in Christ or we're just standing there. Either way, time is passing.

Prophecy can be about a particular issue, but it can also be general. The testimony of Christ is specific, but it is general, as well. If God particularly says, there's going to come a man who's the antichrist, that will certainly come to pass. If God says there will be particular kings and nations that come together and come into covenant with one another and agree to give their power to this man, it will certainly come to pass. Everything that God says in particular about particular things will certainly happen.

Everything that God said about Jesus Christ by the prophets of old certainly happened, even down to being beaten. The prophets of old said the soldiers would cast lots for Jesus' clothes. They said they would pull His beard and spit into His face, and that's exactly what happened. Everything the prophets said about Jesus came to pass.

Everything that God particularly speaks about is for one special reason—to glorify Christ. Why is the antichrist coming? Because Jesus Christ is coming in the clouds and the world is going to see a difference between the true and false prophets. Why does all this evil happen in the world? Because Jesus Christ is coming in glory, power, and might with all His holy angles, and He's going to wipe it all out. The world will see the glory and majesty of Jesus Christ. It's for no other reason. Everything God speaks is for that one reason.

In the same way, everything I preach to you is not anything about myself, but it's for the glory of Jesus Christ in you. Everything I say is according to the testimony of Jesus Christ for His glory in you and me. Paul said, "This is the secret that's been revealed, the mystery that's been kept hidden all these years is Christ in you the hope of glory" (Colossians 1:27).

What is prophecy? It's Christ in you the hope of glory. It's the hope of a better life, better things to come. It's the hope of victory, healing, salvation, the hope of the Holy Spirit, the hope of God's gifts. It's the hope of the growth of the church. It's the hope of everything God can do in me, through me, and for me in Christ Jesus. Everything God speaks has to do with the glory of Jesus Christ. Prophetic—you can't get any more prophetic than that!

Why is God so concerned about you and me? Because every little thing in our lives has to do with our growth—life, mind, spirit, and heart. Every situation you're in concerns God because it concerns you. All of your troubles affect you, and God is concerned about you. But even though our little problems seem big to us, they aren't anything to God. He's not so much concerned about the problems as He is you. You can be overwhelmed with circumstances, and God is most concerned about your spirit, heart, and mind.

Where is your mind? Your heart? Spirit? Thoughts? Where is your faith? Who are you trusting in? Who are you looking to?

I don't know about you, but I'm looking to Jesus! *He* is my hope; *He* is my salvation. *He* is my wisdom, knowledge, my preaching, my spirit. Now, you talk about prophecy. Jesus said, "When the Holy Spirit comes, He's going to tell you everything that I said and remind you. And not only is He going to remind you what I said to you already, but He's also going to teach you things you haven't heard yet and show you things to come." That's prophecy!

What are those things to come? We don't know, but whatever they are, they're in Christ. *We* are all in Christ, and everything that God allows to come is all because we are in Him. He's got everything in His hands, and He has the knowledge of all things. There are many

37

things we don't understand; we can't even comprehend it all. But He's going to show us. He's going to make us understand. He'll clear our minds and fill our hearts. The Holy Ghost is going to make all these things clear to us.

God's not going to leave us in the dark about anything. That's what He means by prophecy. Every once in a while, you need to hear a word from God. And God will send someone to speak a special word to you because He knows you need that.

But that's not the only thing you need. God's only doing that to let you know what this person is saying is what I've been saying to you all along. Everything the preacher is saying to you is what I've been preaching to you your whole lifetime. The Holy Ghost has been speaking the same thing all along, if we'll just listen to Him. There's nothing new under the sun. Solomon said that.

Everything God says is for our growth and encouragement. Encouragement means to move from one place to another—up not down, outward not inward. When somebody is being encouraged, they're not sliding backward; they are being pressed forward. Everything prophetic is forward, going toward the future. All the knowledge we achieve, the knowledge and understanding that God gives us through the Holy Spirit brings us forward step by step.

What is the reason for that? The first reason is to give us strength in the Lord and in the power of His might. Paul said that. I believe Paul was telling us to be fighters, maybe soldiers—big strong fierce men, in the Lord. We should be fierce and stand our ground in Christ. Don't back down; don't give in; don't quit.

Jesus is the head of the Church; He is the one in whom we live and move. He is the one in whom we grow. He is the standard by which we are measured. God put all these in the church: pastors, teachers, prophets, apostles, evangelists for the perfecting of the saints, edifying of the saints, for our building up until we all come unto the stature of that perfect man—Jesus Christ. Until then, we have God's prophecy through the people of His Church.

Chapter 4

True Freedom

The human spirit needs one thing more than anything—freedom. Jesus knew that, and that's why He came, why the Father sent Him. Without freedom the human spirit is depressed, unfruitful, stagnant, and dead. Jesus said, "If you continue in my word, then are you my disciples indeed. And you will know the truth, and the truth will make you free" (John 8:31-32).

Freedom. Does the world really know what freedom is? There are many kinds of freedom. Liberty can be defined by doing what we want to do when we want to do it. We live in a free land. Some countries are not as free as others. And there are many other ideas of what "freedom" means.

But the kind of freedom Jesus gives is the freedom we all need. This is the kind all men are longing for. Let me tell you what I mean.

Jesus set us free civilly so we can freely worship God and serve Him without adversity. But for many places on this earth that's not the case. The enemy is always encroaching on the world like a lion ready to devour and destroy. Satan doesn't want us to be free. And any way he can bring men into bondage, that's what he's working for.

Men can't see they're born in bondage under the reign of Satan. They're born as slaves to sin and darkness of this world. When Jesus came, He set men free from the bondage of sin and the darkness of this world. So, I began to think about what the scripture says about freedom and liberty.

First, the scripture speaks of law and freedom in grace. Paul said, "Stand fast therefore in the liberty wherewith Christ has made us free, be not entangled again with the yoke of bondage" (Galatians 5:1). Jesus said, "Come unto me all ye that labor and heavy laden and I will give you rest. Take my yoke upon you and learn of me" (Matthew 11:28-29). So, the freedom we have in Christ, first of all, makes us free from the law of Moses and the law of sin and death.

Second, Jesus gives us freedom of the spirit and mind. That's more than civil liberty. It's the freedom that only Christ can give. Man can't have lasting satisfying freedom on his own. Without Christ, man can't be totally fulfilled or happy in his life. Everyone in the world is yoked to the spirit of the world, but Jesus said He came to set you from the yoke that binds you. In exchange, though, Jesus says, I want to place *my* yoke upon you. I want you to be bonded with me because I'm the only true liberty there is.

We're just like everybody else. We're all linked by the burden of this world, and we can't seem to escape it. We're a part of it. We have to live in it. So, when we've lived so many years and gone through so much, we grow tired and try to find a means of escape to find some rest and peace of mind. We go fishing or on vacation or go camp by the river. We try to get our minds off the problems and pressures of life.

But we soon find out that's not true freedom because when that's all over, we're right back where we were before—weighted down, stressed out. And we're burdened knowing that we've got to face it all again, go through another day, another year. We want to know, "God, how long is this going to last? How can I put up with this life? Can I get myself free from all this?"

You think, "If I can just be free, I'll be happy." Some people give up all obligations, even all their family. They leave behind everything and everyone that counted on them. But instead of finding true freedom, they just add to their problems. They can't seem to find true peace anywhere. And this is where Jesus comes into the picture.

Jesus came to give us freedom within this world, and He can do that because He overcame the world. He brings with Him the peace and the joy of heaven and sets the soul flying in the heavenlies. He raises the soul and spirit of man out of depression and the oppression of life and sets him free. Hallelujah! And Jesus puts within his soul freedom, cutting him loose from all that binds and the chains that hold his life down.

40

Brother, the world doesn't know this. The world has one definition of freedom, but the only true freedom is in Christ!

Have you ever dreamed of flying? One night, I dreamed the Lord picked me up, and suddenly I rose up from the ground and started flying. I felt the love of God so strong. I knew it was the power of His great love that was causing me to fly. It was the engine and the fuel. And you talk about freedom … It was peace—sweet perfect unspeakable peace. The freedom of God is peace!

It doesn't matter where you are or what situation or circumstance you're in. It doesn't matter where you live or what country you're in. It doesn't matter your financial circumstance. You are free in the midst of it all. God set you free in the lion's den. God set you free in the fiery furnace. God sets you free in the life you think there's no use living anymore. Jesus suddenly gives you a reason for living because you're free in Him. Your mind, soul, spirit, heart … everything about you is free. There are no ties that bind. No spirit in this world has a hold on you.

I spoke to the Lord about His freedom. I said, "Lord, your word talks about being free from the law. But, Lord, if a man's spirit and mind are bound and oppressed, and he's in depression, it doesn't matter whether he's under the law or not. He's bound; he's not free. What about this man?"

The Lord gave me a scripture from the book of Acts. It says, "God anointed Jesus of Nazareth who went about doing good and healing all that were oppressed of the devil, for God was with Him'" (Acts 10:38). God said, "My intention and work is to set men free totally, from every oppression of the enemy. It's not just to set you free from your work schedule or the hum drum of life and give you vacations, destinations, and large sums of money. That's not freedom. That's only a temporary fix. Jesus came to make a permanent fix, real change." He said, "I didn't come just to make them temporarily happy. I came to make them free from every oppression of the enemy."

So, no matter the pressures of life, greater is He that's in you than he that's in the world. That's freedom.

I think we've lost sight on what it means to be free. I remember my dear mother. She'd always talk about that. That was one of her favorite sayings. She said it all the time. "You need to be free," she'd say. "God wants you to be free." She prayed for people or talked with people at church, and she'd say, "The Lord wants to make you free. There's nothing wrong with letting go."

What happens to a man who is set free from a hard disease in his physical body? What does he do? He turns loose, lets go, and gets happy. Suppose a man was born blind and suddenly the Lord opened his eyes, and he can see for the first time. How do you think the man would act? He wouldn't just walk around saying, "Oh, I can see, gee whiz." It's emotions I'm talking about. You would know that something happened to this man because he would be happy!

So it is with a man's soul when the spirit of the Lord comes into our lives and makes us free. That's what Jesus came to do. He came to die, yes. He came to take our place and pay for the penalty of sin. He did all that. But for what? To make us free!

And what are we free from? We're free from every oppression of the enemy. Free from sin, death, and curse of the law. We're free from condemnation and accusation. We're free from the pressures of life in the soul. We're free from the enemy and the chains that bind us, from strongholds and all that wants to hold us down. Things that want to hold us down hold us back, keep us blind, keep us ignorant.

God wants to break those binds and let us experience all that He is, to experience His goodness. He wants to set us free from sin and the bondage of the enemy. He wants to set us free from every oppression, every depression that comes in life.

No matter where we live. No matter what condition of life. People live in the worst conditions and the best conditions, and they're still bound. People are still blind and in the darkness. People in America have the best things in life, and they're the most wretched and miserable people in the world. They can spend all the money they want to spend. They can buy all the things they want to buy to their heart's content. They can purchase everything that they want in life, thinking this is going to finally fulfill their life, and they're still miserable.

Do you know why? Because they're not really free. They are bound by their money and lusts. They're bound by their own selfish ways. They're bound by doubts and fears. And that's why Jesus came to give us new life. It's not the same kind of life we had before, but a new life of liberty, free from everything that's holding us down.

That's why when we come together as Christians to worship God, we should feel free. There should be no ties that bind us. There should be no formula or program we follow. If that's what we do, we've forgotten all about freedom. We have forgotten about the free spirit.

Did you know that God is a free spirit? Nothing binds Him down. Nothing holds God. Is there anything that restrains God? Is there anything that dictates to God or teaches Him? Is there anything that God withdraws from? No! He is free. He is totally and absolutely free.

Think about that. There's nothing that can hold God in, bind Him, or keep Him in. He is everywhere at the same time. His presence fills the universe and the earth. His spirit is everywhere. David said, "If I make my bed in hell behold you are there" (Psalm 139:8). Time, space, or distance cannot hold God back. All things are subject to Him. God created all things, and He dictates them. All things are upheld by the word of His power and are subservient to Him.

And Jesus wants to impart to you this spirit of freedom. That doesn't mean everything is going to be subservient to us, but God is going to see to it that nothing in heaven and earth can hold you back from doing His will. Nothing will keep you from knowing or experiencing Him.

There's no power in heaven or earth that's big enough to stop what God intends to do in your life, what He creates in your soul and spirit. Hallelujah. He makes you free.

If you're a Christian, and you don't feel that freedom, it's your own heart that's holding you back. If you don't feel that freedom, it's your own spirit binding you. God wants us to realize He has made us free.

You might say, "Oh Lord, if I just had enough money, then I believe I would be satisfied and my life fulfilled." That's not a free spirit. That's putting yourself under bondage, under obligation. That's a person who has forgotten he's been made free. A person like that doesn't want to live free, talk free, worship free, or act free.

What does God want of us? He wants us to be free with the idea that nothing binds, nothing holds. There's nothing impossible with God. I'm a child of God, and I have access into this grace wherein I stand. I can come before my Father anytime day or night. I have freedom to talk with Him. I'm free as the wind, as a bird.

Look outside and see the birds flying. You might say, "Oh, I wish I could be like that." You desire to be like that in your spirit because Jesus made you to long for freedom. When it's all said and done, we'll have even greater freedom than the birds.

The liberty we have in Christ can't be taken away. It'll never stop. It'll never die. The birds will die. The beasts will die. The things we think are free will die. The mountains and scenery are beautiful, and we take in all that beauty and grandeur, and it just does something to our souls. But after a while, those things are going to pass away.

There's an experience with God that surpasses anything on earth. His word will never pass away. He said, "You will know the truth and the truth will make you free forever more" (John8:32). Think about that. When the stars are falling from heaven, you'll be soaring like an eagle for Jesus.

So, let's not think of ourselves as one that's bound up—can't move, can't speak, can't do. God does not want us to be concerned about how and what and when we do what He's called us to do. He just wants us just to stay on the thoughts of freedom. Paul said, "Stand fast" (Philippians 1:4-9). That means don't let go, hold your ground, be firm, be unmovable. Don't let the enemy lie to you, deceive you, and trick you. But stand fast on the word of God.

God wants a free people because when we're free, there ain't nothing we can't do if we're free in Him. There's not a mountain too big, a valley too low. There's not a fire too hot, not a river too wide. There's not anything too deep or wide for us when we're free.

Take free people in the civil sense, like we have in America. If you make people free of tyrannical government, there are no limits to what that people can do because they are free. They are given the privilege and opportunity to achieve, work, build, and create. That's what happens in a free society.

God wants us to be a free society, but more than that, He wants our souls to be free. Money can't buy our freedom. Opportunity can't buy our freedom. Jesus purchased our freedom at the cross, and now He gives it to us freely!

When you find that freedom, you'll know the difference. It shows up when we get down to pray and seek the Lord. Suddenly we feel that free spirit—the Holy Spirit, moving in our hearts. We know when it's just a cut and dry prayer, and when it's the real thing. Don't you want the real thing?

If I don't have true freedom in Christ, all the preaching I do is not going to make me free. All the singing I do is not going to make me free. I can't do *anything* to make myself free. But when Christ makes me free, I sing because I'm happy. I sing because I'm free.

Is that why you sing? Is that why you shout because you're free? Is that why you come to church and worship and sing to the Lord? We're free because Jesus made us free. I can get up here and talk about the old days and how people used to shout and praise God, jump up and down, run around the pews and run outside and swing around the pole, and everything else. But do you know why they did those things? Because they felt a depth of freedom that only Jesus can give. They no longer felt hindered by the looks and judgements of others.

Once it happens inside of you, there ain't no telling what you might do, hallelujah. I've seen people who didn't believe in all that shouting, whooping, and carrying on. Then suddenly something happens to them. They get so happy in their soul, they start praising God, crying, and shouting all at the same time. They're so happy they don't know what to do or what to say. They start jumping up and down, running, or whatever they can do to try to express the freedom they feel.

When we get to heaven, we're finally going to be totally free from all the darkness in this earth. This flesh will drop off, and we won't have to contend with sickness or sin anymore. It'll be all gone. Free at last, free at last, thank God almighty we're free at last.

When Peter went down to Cornelius' house and the spirit came upon them, and they spoke with tongues, imagine how Cornelius' household felt at the time (Acts 10:25). But where the spirit of the Lord is there is liberty. You may speak in tongues; you may not. You may shout; you may not. You may cry; you may not. You may fold your hands and pray, or you may not even raise your hands. There's no telling what you may do, but throughout your lifetime you'll do something because you no longer feel hindered by the judgement of man.

Something powerful takes place when you live in freedom. The way you talk, the way you think, what motivates you, what you love and desire, what you dedicate yourself to. You feel free to do whatever it is that God's called you to do.

Like my friend, Brother Tom. He says he loves playing with the praise team. Do you know why? He's not all bound up in himself. God's freedom makes him eager to serve. He's eager to do the work of God.

When you live free in the Spirit you know God's in control, and everything's good. There's no worry. When we live in the spirit, we are free to proclaim the word, to help, do, and be like Jesus. We are free to walk with Jesus and to know Him. We are free to believe, ask anything, walk, and talk. We are free to worship, have knowledge, wisdom, and faith. We are free to have joy, peace, mercy, and love. And all these good things of God are free to us.

All these free gifts begin to generate and produce. They begin to show themselves in a free people. Somebody might say, "I can't love. I wish I could." Well, get free, and you *will* love. Somebody might say, "I don't know … I can't forgive that person." Well, get free, and you *will* forgive that person. Somebody might say, "I can't sing like that. I can't worship." Yes, you can! Get free, and you will. No matter what your voice sounds like, you'll want to sing for Jesus. I've heard people that couldn't carry a tune in a bucket start singing, and the sweet presence of the Lord filled the air.

I don't know if you've seen the movie *Braveheart*, about the Scottish hero William Wallace. Do you remember when they finally caught him in the end? They were going to do what they call "quarter" him. They laid him on the table to torture him. They thought by threatening his life he would give into the king and renounce everything he believed. But instead, with his last breath he cried out, "Freedom!"

William Wallace was talking about being free from the tyranny of evil. He longed for the Scotts to be a free people. But those of us who know Christ, we have the same cry. Freedom should be the cry of every member of the body of Christ. Christ already paid the price. He already died and overcame death. We cried out for liberty, and the Lord said, "I give you liberty because I died for liberty. It's yours."

It should be the cry of the church today. Lord, make us free. Make us free in heart, spirit, soul, and mind. Where your spirit is there is liberty.

Father, in the name of Jesus, I ask you to let us always to be mindful of this. You are that great free spirit, and where you dwell, in whom you inhabit, there is liberty. Help us Lord, to know that we are a liberated people. We're free, oh God, we're free. If there's something troubling us or holding us back, Lord, help us to reach out to you. Father, make every spirit free this morning, in Jesus' name.

Chapter 5

The Imperishable Blood of Jesus

The blood of Jesus—that's what's been on my heart and mind the last few days. There's much to think about the precious blood of Jesus. There are some facts I want to share with you that are interesting to me, things I've read about.

There's an explorer named Ron Wyatt. He died about twelve years ago or so, a Christian man. He did a lot of digging on his own in the Bible lands, searching for artifacts related to the Bible. He loved God, so he sought the Lord for his guidance. He didn't have an organization behind him. He had a job, but he spent a lot of his years traveling throughout the Bible lands over there.

Wyatt found several things I believe are genuine. But one of the most interesting things he said he found was the Ark of the Covenant. He said the Lord lead him to the place where it was hidden. He said he found it about 20 feet below the place where he believed Jesus was crucified.

History had lost the whereabouts of the Ark for all these thousands of years. After the invasion of Jerusalem, in the time of the prophets, the Ark was hidden for safe keeping. So, no one knew where it was. But Wyatt believed he found it.

He dug through the mountain where Jesus was crucified, down through holes and caves and pulled out debris and rocks. And he came to an ancient room where he found the Ark. White said he scraped off some of the blood that covered the Ark. He took it back to civilization and had it analyzed.

The blood had flowed down from the cross, through a crack in the rocks directly above the Ark. The evidence of the broken rock is backed up by scripture. If you'll remember, the gospel of Matthew says there was a great earthquake when Jesus died, and the rocks rent (Matthew 27:51).

When Wyatt had the blood analyzed, they discovered the blood wasn't actually dead. It was alive. You see, dead blood can't give a chromosome count, but they could get it from this blood. And the results dumbfounded the experts. They explained this blood only had half the number of chromosomes of normal blood. Most of the chromosomes were from the female, and only one was from a male. But the male chromosome wasn't from a human.

The experts asked White, "Where did you get this blood? Whose blood is it?" He cried and said, "It's the blood of your Messiah."

Watching the video shook me up. And that's what I want to talk to you about today—the blood of Jesus. When God made Adam, the Bible says He made all men of one blood. In other words, we all came from Adam. But our blood is corrupt. Since sin came into the world, our blood is defiled. Don't ask me how, but somehow in the spirit world when Adam sinned it brought death and corruption into the physical world. So, everything we see in the physical world is dying and decaying. Nothing in the flesh goes on living forever.

But when Jesus came, we know He was not born of man. He was born of a *woman*, but he did not *come* from woman. He was born of the Holy Spirit that overshadowed Mary. So His blood didn't come from man. He didn't come from Adam. Jesus' blood wasn't decayed and defiled. It was pure and holy, and alive.

I begin to think about that blood. One drop of Jesus' blood is enough to cleanse us and make us whole. Just one drop of His blood is powerful and holy enough to save the whole world. But Jesus *poured out* His blood when He was beaten and crucified.

God determined to do this from the very beginning of the world. Jesus was the lamb slain from the foundation of the world. And the blood of Jesus has brought mercy. In Hebrews 12:18-24, the scripture says:

> You're not come to the mount that might be touched and burned with fire or blackness and darkness and tempest and sound of the trumpet and the voice of words which voice they heard and trusted, that the word would not be spoken to them

anymore. They could not endure that which was commanded that so much as a beast touched this mountain it will be stoned or thrust through with a dart. So terrible was the sight that Moses said, I exceedingly fear and quake. But you are not come unto Mt Zion. Ah, but ye are come to Mt Zion and to the city of the living God. The heavenly Jerusalem to an innumerable company of angels, to the general assembly and church of the first born which are written in heaven and to God the judge of all and the spirits of just men made perfect and to Jesus the mediator of the New Covenant and to the blood of sprinkling that speaketh better things than that of Abel.

Why does the writer talk about Cain and Abel here? The great reformer Martin Luther translated the name Cain from Hebrew as, "I have the man, the Lord." So, Luther believed Cain's name was a message from God, a promise to give man a redeemer. God promised when Adam and Eve sinned that, even though Satan would bruise the Redeemer's heal, Jesus would crush the serpent's head.

So, I began to look at the other name, Abel. His name actually means "vanity of vane." It means "unsatisfactory." But how could that be? The Bible says when Abel offered up his sacrifice he was accepted of God, but Cain's offering was rejected.

That's when a thought came to me. You see, Abel realized that in himself, he is not the Lord. He knew he was not the conqueror of life. He knew in himself he was nothing—vanity of vanities (as Solomon said) and unsatisfactory to God. So, by faith Abel offered up sacrifice and worshipped God, and God counted his sacrifice and his faith as righteousness.

Cain, on the other hand, thought, "I'm a man. I'm the lord of my life, and I'll do what I please." God rejected that.

Getting back to Hebrews, the Bible says the blood of Jesus Christ speaks better things than Abel. I began to wonder what that meant. After the sacrifices offered up, Cain rose up against his brother. He was angry because his sacrifice was rejected and his brother's was accepted. So, Cain killed his brother in the field.

We know the story. After a while, the Lord came to Cain and said, "Why has your countenance fallen? If you do well, you'll be accepted. If you don't, sin lies at the door." The Lord said, "Where's your brother?" And Cain responded, "I don't know. Am I my brother's keeper?" And the Lord said, "What have you done? The blood of your brother cries unto me from the ground. Cursed be Cain," God said, and drove Cain out into the wilderness (Genesis 4:8-11).

What was the blood of Abel crying out to God for? It's crying out for judgment. Abel wanted revenge against his brother. After all, Able was a righteousness man, and Cain was a murderer. Abel believed in God, and Cain rejected God.

But when Jesus came and shed His blood, spilling it upon the ground for you and me, it wasn't crying out for vengeance. It was crying out, "Lord, have mercy upon these people!" The blood of Jesus Christ speaks better things than that of Abel, because it cries out for our redemption. It cries out for God to be merciful and gracious to us.

Abel was a righteousness man. He counted himself as nothing when he offered up his sacrifice. He knew he was vain and worthless, but he gave his best to God, and God received it.

When Jesus died offered up Himself, He a man without spot or blemish. He was perfect in all His ways. And when my sins killed Him, when my sins put Him on that cross, His blood didn't say, "Father, take vengeance on this wrathful people and pour your wrath on the world." He said, "Father, I give my life because I want you to give them mercy and eternal life." When His blood cried out, the Father heard and was pleased.

Now I want to refer to a passage starting at Leviticus 17:11. When God gave Moses the law of sacrifice and explained to him what he should do, God said, "For the life of the flesh is in the blood, and I have given to you upon the altar to make an atonement for your souls." It is the blood that makes an atonement for the soul.

Now refer back to Hebrews 9, starting in verse 7:

> The priest goes in once a year, not without blood that he offers for himself and for the errors of the people. The Holy Ghost signifying that the way to the holiest of all was not yet manifest while the first tabernacle was standing. It was a figure for the time presence in which were offered gifts and sacrifices that could not make him that did the service perfect, pertaining to the conscious. It stood only in meats and drinks and washings and carnal ordinances and poles for them for the time of reformation. But Christ becoming high priest of good things to come by a greater and more perfect tabernacle not made with

hands, that is to say not of this building, neither by the blood of goats and cows but by His own blood. He entered in once into the holy place, having obtained eternal redemption for us. For if the blood of bulls and goats and ashes of an heifer sprinkling the unclean sanctifies the purifying of the flesh, how much more shall the blood of Christ who through the eternal spirit offered Himself without spot to God, purge your conscience from dead works to serve the living God.

So, what is so special about the blood of Jesus? First, it didn't come from Adam. It's not of this earth. We're talking about something literal. It's not just a fairytale. When Jesus walked on this earth, He was a man just like you and me. The Bible says the word was made flesh. But He was not sinful flesh. He was a man in all points like we are, yet without sin. He was even tempted as we are, yet without sin. His blood was not tainted or corrupt. His blood was pure.

What does that mean for us? Well, God said, the life is in the blood. Every person without Christ, they may be up walking around, but they're dead while they live. There is no life in those without Christ. The life that comes from Adam is corrupt.

But men busy themselves and worry about all the concerns of life. And all along, they're missing the most important part of life—the life that's in Christ. That's a life that's not of this world.

It makes me angry when the government spends billions of dollars, claiming they are giving all we need to sustain life. And they always leave out the most important thing in life! They claim they can't mix church and state. So, religion and spirituality become the least they're concerned about.

The elite in the country promote what they say is important to life, while they rob, cheat, lie, and steal. We need to feed the spirit man, not just the physical man. The spirit man is what Christ came for. He said the carnal came first. He's talking about Adam—the blood in our veins and our flesh. That's the carnal.

And then the second Adam came from heaven—Jesus. Did He come just to fix our physical need? Did He come to create a new government for the welfare of the people? No! He came to give us a new heart. He came so we could be born again!

I'm not saying God's not concerned about our physical needs. God wants to bless us, in the spirit and in the flesh, and He will bless us. He *has* blessed us. Praise God. We're living in Canaan's land right now. The Lord said, "Open your eyes and look; it's there for you to have. Take it."

The world couldn't understand what Jesus came to do. He walked among His own, and His own didn't receive Him. The Jews hated Him. But He didn't come to fit in and be liked. He didn't come to look like every other man. God made Adam in His image. But when Jesus came, He recreated what it meant to be made in God's image. The first man fell, but this next man—He's going to stand forever.

The glory of Adam was wonderful, but the glory of Jesus Christ exceeds the glory of all mankind. I hear people say, "When Jesus comes back, God will restore everything, and everything will be back to the Garden of Eden." I hope not. I think it's going to be greater than Eden! Jesus talked about a place He is preparing for us, and I believe it's far beyond anything in this world.

The place God creates for those who love Him, those He's coming for, it will never pass away. It will endure forever and ever and far exceed anything the world has ever known. So, I would rather rejoice and be exceedingly glad in the glory of Christ than to ever think I would go back to the glory of Adam.

Adam brought with him a beautiful creation. But Jesus brings with Him a greater glory than anything we see in the sun, moon, stars, trees, water, and flowers. We can't imagine that! I can't think of anything more beautiful than the Rocky Mountains or a setting sun on a South Pacific island. Could there be anything more glorious than that? Oh, you better believe there is! We just haven't seen anything like it yet. We're on our way, friends, and one day we're going to see Jesus as He is in all His glory.

Jesus is coming. The world's about to see a glory it's never known before. And the blood of Jesus is what gets us there! The life is in the blood. It reaches to the highest mountain, flows to the lowest valley. The blood will never lose its power, never lose its life. You can't kill it; it won't die; it won't decay, it won't rot.

When God sees the blood of Jesus flowing in us, His wrath will pass us over. God will say, "You will never die because *my* blood flows in your veins." I'm talking about a blood you don't see. I'm talking about a life the world can't put under a microscope.

The blood I'm talking about is not mystical. I'm talking about something tangible; you can feel it. If I had one drop of His blood in my hand right now, that blood would never die. The Bible says, "My holy one will not see corruption."

Jesus was born a man, died a man, and rose as a man. He's not going to lose that human part. We're not talking about Jesus being a mystical spirit. The body Jesus had before He died wasn't corrupt because He never sinned. On His own, Jesus would have never died. His sinless humanity would have spared Him from death, just like it *would* have saved Adam.

So, why did Jesus hang on the cross? He became corrupt by taking our sins upon Himself. The Bible says He became sin. He just didn't take on our sin; He became sin. Every murderer, liar, thief, you name it, Jesus took on that sin. Start with yourself. Make a list of all your sins—all the past and present darkness of your heart. Jesus became that sin for you. That's why He died.

Jesus offered His life and His blood to God. He said, "My life, Father, I offer to you. The life that I am, the life that I have, the righteousness I am, I offer to you." He offered up His life, and what was His life? The life was in the blood.

Jesus' body was covered with our sins. His body was beaten, scourged, whipped, and torn beyond recognition. Jesus' body was traumatized. His joints were pulled apart. Yet He was battling with the armies of darkness.

God sent His most precious pearl to defeat the darkness of sin and shame, wickedness, and ungodliness. It wasn't Adam's blood that saved us. He couldn't live a righteous life. Only Jesus could do what Adam could not. Jesus said, "He that believes in me shall have eternal life" (John 3:16). All He has is ours, and the life in Him is in us.

The Bible says, "Flesh and blood shall not enter into the kingdom of heaven" (1 Corinthians 15:50). That's referring to Adam's flesh and blood. What Adam gave us won't be there. That corrupt blood can't make it. There's no life in it; it's dead. But there is a fountain that flows, hallelujah.

It makes me want to sing the old hymn: "What can wash away my sin? Nothing but the blood of Jesus. What can make me whole again? Nothing but the blood of Jesus. Oh precious is that flow that makes me white as snow. No other fount I know. Nothing but the blood of Jesus."

Jesus knew what He had to do to take all our sins. He volunteered to take all the darkness of the world upon His shoulders. When the devil thought he finally killed Jesus and shut Him up forever, all he did was open up the doors for eternity.

And that blood is still there before God. No blood was good enough to be before God, except the blood of Jesus. That's what gave me the right to stand before God. I am what I am—corrupt. But God sent another life—one that was uncorrupt and imperishable—to give His blood for me. When a person comes to Christ, the Holy Spirit covers your spirit and washes you. The blood is what makes you clean.

The word says, "Let us draw near with a true heart in full assurance, having boldness to enter into the holiest by the blood of Jesus" (Hebrews 10:22). They had animal sacrifices in the Old Testament. Wasn't sin removed because the animal died? No, because that blood wasn't good enough. The sin of man had to be covered by the blood of man. But not just any man. It had to be a perfect man.

It was a blood covenant, an eternal promise between God and man. And Jesus didn't just pour out a few drops. He emptied His life. We don't want to think about the grim scene. It's terrible to think about. The floor was covered. They nailed Him to the cross. The cross was bloody.

And here the word tells us to come boldly to the throne of grace, having this confidence in the blood. You and I need to remember that. We need to see Jesus in all His blood. We need to see that sacrifice. It wasn't easy. He not only suffered for us, but He did it generously. God didn't give us a little assurance; He gave us a great assurance.

There's enough blood for you and me. There's enough blood for everybody. There's enough blood for every need to be met and to save every soul. It's enough to set every captive free. God didn't make it short. He fills our cup overflowing.

Jesus became what you are on that cross, so you and I can become what He is. Hallelujah. Jesus is offering you His righteousness. Why is my son my son? Because he has my blood. *My* blood. I'm his father because he has my blood flowing in his veins. Jesus said, "I'll make you just like me because my blood is in you."

My sons and my daughter know they can come to me anytime. They have confidence because they are in the blood line. They're kin folk. In the same way, the church is family because we all share the same blood—the blood of Jesus. Think about it, saints. Meditate on it day and night.

I used to grow up with some folks who would say, "Hey, blood," when they saw close friends and family. And that's what we're going to hear from Jesus one day. He's going to say, "Hey, blood, come on in!"

We have confidence in Jesus for one reason only. I have the right to come to Him because of His blood. It covers me; I'm enveloped in it. I'm born again of it. And if I'm in the family of God, all the promises of God are mine. His inheritance is mine. I have a blood right.

I want you to pray this: Father, thank you for the precious blood of Jesus that was poured out for me. Through Him I have access to you for all of my needs, which will be supplied according to your riches in glory by Christ Jesus. Father, thank you for the privilege in Jesus name.

There are literally preachers in churches today that are trying to blot out and dismiss the blood from the Bible and their messages. But without it, we have no hope. Trust in His blood; trust in His assurance. There's nothing the blood can't do if you trust Him.

Chapter 6

Come Out of the Shadows

I love the words of that old Christmas song, "Oh little town of Bethlehem how still we see thee lie. Above thy deep and dreamless sleep, the silent stars go by. Yet in thy dark street shineth the everlasting light. The hopes and fears of all the years are met in thee tonight."

Christmas songs have the most beautiful compositions of the gospel. There are no other songs in the world more beautiful. Yet today across the world, and in America of all places, some want to dismiss these songs from the public square. But never from our hearts shall His light be extinguished. We, the children of God, shall stand firm, and the attack on Christ will one day cease.

Today, the world is living in the "shadows" of Christ. Every man who believes in God and comes to Him, once lived in His shadow. Israel, being under the law of Moses, were living in the shadows of Christ. Every time they offered up a burnt offering or a sacrifice or took part in a ritual of worship, they were only worshipping God in shadows.

Hebrews 10:1 says, "The law, having a 'shadow' of good things to come but not the very image of the things, can never with those sacrifices which they offered year by year continually, make the comers thereunto perfect." Hebrews 8:5 says, "If Jesus were on earth, He would not be priest seeing that there are priests that offer according to the law, who serve unto the examples and 'shadows' of heavenly things, as Moses was admonished of God. When he was about to make the tabernacle he said, 'Make all things according to the pattern shown to you on the mountain.' But we know that whatever things the pattern was, was only a shadow of the real substance."

What is shadow? If you hold up something in the light it casts a shadow. It is a witness, you might say, to what is real. A world without Christ lives in the witness of His reality. Sadly, they are satisfied there. They hear about Him and talk about Him but have not come to see Him clearly. They only see a shadow of Him.

In Ephesians Paul prayed for us to be enlightened, that we would grow in the knowledge of Jesus, not head knowledge, but heart knowledge. Only the heart can see Jesus. Christ is knowledge to the spirit of man, the eyes of his understanding. Christ brings the reality of God to the heart. He shares with us in His fullness, so that we actually come to know God in Him.

There are people who don't know God but can tell you all about Him. They can quote the scripture chapter and verse, but they have never come into the light of God. You can know about God, but never experience Him. It's like a country boy who never came to the city. He read about it, but never experienced it.

Matthew 4:15-16 says, "The land of Zebulon and the land of Naphthalin, by the way of the sea, beyond Jordan, Galilee of the gentiles; the people which sat in darkness saw great light; and to them which sat in the region and 'shadow' of death light is sprung up."

Someone may ask, "Who is Jesus, and what is He all about?" Jesus Christ is the light of this world from heaven. The whole world was shut up in the darkness of sin and law, until Christ came. All that was foretold of Him, testified to a new day, a new thing that God would do on the earth. All of life foreshadowed this coming. Until He appeared, there was only the shadow of Him.

Men did not understand the salvation that Christ would bring. It wasn't made totally clear. Then Jesus came, the light of man. He showed God's promise. Christ was the light of life, and the darkness of men could not put out His light. This was God's time for man, and man's time for God. Could the earth exist without the warmth and light of the sun? Even when we are in the dark of the night, we are not beyond the sun's effect.

Christ came like the sun, a shining beacon of hope into the darkness of this world. What a contrast. His life was so bright, men began to see how dark their own lives were, no matter how enlightened they thought they were.

Oh, come to the light and walk no more in the darkness of this world. Do you see the light? Walk in it while you have it. Your soul cannot find what it longs for in the darkness, in the shadows of life.

God gives to us the true light of day. The shadows only tell us that there is a loving God. God, who in the beginning said, "Let there be light," He sent His son, Jesus, to bring that light and show men the real meaning and purpose of life. Jesus came to bring us into fellowship with the Father, to experience His shining presence for the first time in our existence.

God has told us that we can now draw near to Him. Now we can hear Him speaking to our hearts. We can know Him in spirit and in truth. We are now partakers of His life, not living in the shadows, but in the light of Him.

Did you ever feel like you were standing on the outside somewhere looking in? Jesus gave us the opportunity to go in. He is the way into the Father. You don't have to stand outside anymore, wishing or hoping for something better in life. Jesus said, "I am the way; I am the door. He that enters in by me shall go in and out and find pasture" (John 10:9). He gives us access to God, into the reality of His presence.

God's presence is more real than we could ever imagine. He is not like the wind blowing here and there, here one minute and gone the next. But God Himself is forever present with us in the Son, and we can walk forever in the light of His countenance. Hallelujah! The true knowledge of God can only be known in Christ, who is the brightness of His glory and the expressed image of His person.

In Hebrews 1:3, Paul said, "I pray that the eyes of your understanding being enlightened in the knowledge of Christ." Paul knew Him, and we can know Christ as well as Paul and the apostles did.

In 1 John 1:3 the apostle says, "That which we have seen and heard we declare unto you, that you also may have fellowship with us; and truly our fellowship is with the Father, and with His son Jesus Christ." We no longer see Him as the flesh sees Him, Paul tells us. But now we know Christ in all things new, as He is in spirit and truth.

Jesus came in the flesh to do a work which had to be done at the cross. But now we know Christ in spirit. I've had people ask, "How do you know God is real? That Jesus is real?" I point and say because

He's right here in my heart. Yes, Jesus lives in me, but also the eyes of my understanding has been enlightened.

How does God make Himself known to us? First, He says, "You are no longer in the night, but in the light." So, faith is the beginning of God is us. Faith is the substance of things hoped for, the evidence of things not seen (Hebrews 11:1). God plants the faith in our hearts.

Faith is what makes us hope for things we don't see. I don't see Jesus with my eyes, but with my faith. The Lord says, "Now you have me." I know He's real in me, because He said He is. Paul is telling us that we grow in the knowledge of Christ as we come to know Christ by faith in His word.

God has made everything clear to our hearts and our minds. It is not wishful thinking. We are not reaching out in the dark, but we stand in the light. Faith, which comes from God, allows us to believe in what God says, and also reassures our hearts before Him.

When Jesus came into the world, people were not reaching out for something that they couldn't see or hear. They were reaching for His light, the light of His compassion. They saw, heard, and they were convinced of His love for them.

In Ephesians 2:8 Paul said "to every man is given the measure of faith. It is the gift of God." But he also said there were some who did not have faith.

In Acts 6, there were seven honest men of good report, full of the Holy Ghost, that were chosen by the apostles, to wait on tables for the widows and the orphans, the poor and needy. Stephen was one of them.

Stephen was full of faith and power and did great wonders among the people. And the rulers of the people could not resist the wisdom and spirit by which he spoke. There was a power at work that could only be understood by those who were in Christ. But it was the wisdom and spirit by which he spoke that troubled the leaders.

Remember, God is spirit and His spirit is light. And the light always exposes what is in the darkness. Jesus said that men loved darkness rather than light because their deeds were evil (John 3:19). When God's light is shining, the devils always cry out, "Leave us alone. What have we to do with you?"

Stephen struck a nerve. Being brought in before the council, he told them how they had not obeyed God but always resisted Him in their hearts. God would manifest Himself to them, but they were "stiff-necked and uncircumcised in their hearts." In a day of light, they had no excuse. A new day dawned as the Morning Star rose.

The spirit of God in the world today is moving and stirring. No man can come to God, except the spirit of God draw him. People will either shy away or come to Christ. They will either get mad or get happy. Some people just brush Jesus off and care not at all.

Man, in his rebellious nature, tries to resist an all-knowing and truthful God. In a way, man hides from God in the shadows. But he really can't hide from God. He may deny God and resist the truth and excuse himself. His pride will not allow him to admit the truth about himself. Until he sees his own desperate need for Christ, he will not come into the light of Christ.

The light of the spirit of God is delivering undeniable truth to minds and hearts. The heart knows when God is speaking. For God is spirit, and so is man, and through the spirit He makes connection with us.

Do you remember what happened to Peter? When the time for Christ's arrest came, Peter fled (Mark 14:50). He followed Jesus for three years. He grew to love Him dearly. Jesus became his best friend. Peter cared for Jesus more than anyone he ever knew. He would have laid down his life for Him. What an impression Jesus had made on Peter.

Together, in the upper room at supper, Jesus told His disciples, "I am going away, and where I go you cannot come. My command to you is love one another as I have loved you" (John 13:31-38). Peter seemed completely oblivious and said, "Lord, where are you going?" Jesus said, "Just as I told the Jews, where I am going you cannot come. But you will follow me afterwards. I want you to love one another as I have loved you."

Jesus is getting straight to the point. He's telling the disciples what He wants them to do. Peter *hears* Jesus, but he's not really listening. Perhaps Peter was thinking, "Alright, love one another, alright. But where are you going, Lord? Wherever it is, I want to go with you!" But Jesus was trying to tell Peter the greater message. "I want you to love one another so that all will know that you are mine."

I want you to see the love Peter has for his Lord. Jesus said, "He who loves me is he who keeps my commandments." Peter's love for Christ was without spiritual understanding. He was driven with blind ambition. Peter says, "I know your love, and I hear what you're saying, but, Lord, what will we do without you?"

Like a child on a tour, Peter didn't want to follow the guide's rules, he wanted to go and see things that were off limits. His zeal would only lead him down a path of bitterness and sorrow. When Jesus said Peter would deny Him, not once, but three times, that was too much for Peter to hear. He was confused and troubled. He wondered how Jesus couldn't see how much he cared for Him.

"Let not your heart be troubled," Jesus said. He was speaking to all, but I believe most sincerely to Peter. "If you believe in God, believe also in me" (John 14:1). Jesus was saying, "Trust me. What I do now, you don't understand, but you will later."

When Jesus was arrested, Peter went on the defense for his Lord. He took up the sword. But remember what the scripture says in 1 Corinthians 10:4, "The weapons of our warfare are not carnal, but mighty through God to the pulling down of strongholds ... and bringing into captivity every thought to the obedience of Christ."

Peter's struggle was not with man or situations, but with himself. When we ignore the leading of the Lord, we run headlong into trouble. "Put it away, Peter," Jesus said. "How will the scriptures be fulfilled if I do not drink this cup?" (John 18:11). Peter had met the Savior of the world, but only considered Him as friend. Peter did not yet know Jesus as Lord and Savior of his soul. Peter knew that Jesus was God's Messiah, so it seemed reasonable that he should fight back.

Remember the words Jesus said to Peter earlier in His ministry. "Get thee behind me, Satan. For you do not savor the things of God, but those of men" (Matthew 16:33). Peter did not understand. His human passion had been awakened, but not his understanding. Peter only knew he must do something.

But like all the rest of the disciples, Peter ended up running for his life. He went out into the darkness of the night and in the confusion of his mind. They took away his Lord, and he was rebuked for trying to stop them. Jesus even healed the soldier's ear when Peter cut it off with his sword.

Willful disobedience does not fit into God's plan. He already knows the end from the beginning. We don't know what to do in some circumstance, but God knows what to do. He has it all in control. As much as we may passionately love Him, let us wait on Him. He will make everything clear to us in time.

When Jesus was arrested, Peter followed afar. He was watching everything from a safe distance, like a coward. But he couldn't stay away. Peter loved Jesus. The rest of the disciples were nowhere to be found. Only John went in the house where the Lord was taken.

It was a very cold night when Jesus was arrested. A fire was made. Peter warmed himself. But can we comfort ourselves outside of Christ? Can we find the true joy of life without Him? There is no life without His presence. There is nothing but an empty shell. The only way we can find satisfaction and peace of mind is through Christ. Only the final work of Jesus could warm Peter's heart and calm his troubled mind.

Being confronted three times, Peter denied even knowing Jesus. Like all men, he was afraid to die. Leaving the house of Caiaphas, Jesus must have looked across the courtyard to Peter, and their eyes met. Instantly, Peter knew and went out and wept bitterly (Matthew 26:75).

I believe the heart of Jesus ached for Peter. He understood Peter's sorrow. Peter's Lord and master had been taken away, and He would surely die. Peter must have cried out, "They are taking my Lord away, and I don't know what to do! I've denied Him! I've denied that I even know Him!" Peter was weeping in the shadows.

Why do so many professing Christians deny knowing Jesus Christ in their everyday life? They haven't really understood what He did. They really don't know His redemptive work. Are they seeking Him? Or are they like Peter, just wandering in the shadows after Him. And they wonder why they're not happy, not satisfied, not content in life. They may see but not understand. Hear, but not conceive.

Jesus knew Peter. He said, "Simon [Peter], Satan has desired to sift you as wheat. But I have prayed for you, that your faith will not fail" (Luke 22:31). Praise be to God! The Savior Himself has petitioned the Father. Don't you know, the Father listens to the prayers of His Son? "O Father, strengthen his faith," Jesus said. "Don't let him slip away. Keep him, Father, in the palm of your hand. Keep my dear Peter from the enemy that would destroy him."

The enemy was coming to Peter, to test his faith with fire. He wanted to bring Peter down to hell. But Jesus prayed for him. And Jesus prays for every one of us. In John 17 Jesus prayed that we would all be made one in Him, and that by this, the world would believe that

God sent Him. So, our continual fellowship with Him is our testimony to the world that He surely lives.

The people in the town asked Peter, "Do you know Jesus?" And he declared, "No, I don't know Him." They pressed in, "Surely you're one of His disciples. I saw you with Him." He said, "No, I don't know the man. No!" The fire was burning in his breast! "No, I don't know Him. You've got the wrong fellow. I may look like somebody you've seen, but I'm not him." But they were not convinced. "Yes … you were with Him. You speak like a Galilean. You're one of His, alright."

The Bible says Peter cursed and swore because of the darkness in his own soul. He was angry because he was following afar, in the shadows. He had distanced himself from Jesus. He has said one thing but reacted another. He had not yet learned to trust the Lord.

If we want to be Jesus' disciples, we must draw near to Him by trusting His word. After all the things Christ taught His disciples, He continued to remind them to trust in Him. When we pull away, our hearts break and our spirits cry out, "Oh Lord, help me. I don't know what to do. Help me!"

Peter went out into the night crying and praying. Jesus went through the trial being mocked and scourged, but He still remembered Peter. He was still on Jesus' heart and mind. Peter was the very reason Jesus allowed all of this to happen to Himself. Christ came to save Peter. He came to save all of us.

Through all Christ suffered, He remembered even me. He went to the cross for me. What do you tell someone that doesn't believe? You might say, "Did you know that one day Jesus was thinking of you? Of you! While you live in this world of darkness occupied with only yourself, like Peter, Jesus was thinking of you."

There are some records that say there were tens of thousands of people there that day beholding Jesus upon the cross. Did they know why He suffered so much? They were close to Him, and yet so far away. Could Christ reach them? Could He reach the multitudes, like He did during His ministry, and bring them to redemption?

How many beheld Christ on the cross, and yet remained in the darkness about Him? Just as surely as the darkness came over the land that day, so shall the light of His glory and grace brightly shine upon everyone who keeps their eyes and hearts upon Him.

When the women brought news that Jesus was raised from the dead, John and Peter ran together to the sepulcher. John stopped on the outside looking in, but Peter came running up, and passing John, went into the tomb. At last, Peter was coming out of the shadows, and into the light of resurrection.

There was no more weeping, no more sorrow, a certain excitement filled the air and began to fill Peter's heart. "He's not here! He has risen!" Death could not hold Jesus. The darkness of this world cannot extinguish the light of His glory! The hearts of the disciples began to stir, and the life that is Christ became theirs! Just as surely as He lives, He lives within their hearts, and He will never die again!

When Christ has risen in your hearts, you will begin to really live. He will fill your lives to overflowing. For everything about Jesus is soul filling and soul stirring. If you feel a tug in your hearts, that's Him. If you meet a stranger on the Jericho road walking beside you freely bearing your load, that's Him! If somebody wakes you in the middle of the night and says, "I need you," that's Him! That man of Galilee whose blood was shed for thee. If He fills your cup up to the brim, that's Him; that's Him!

How do I know Jesus lives? Because He awakened me out of the slumber of myself and filled my innermost being with His love and grace. Oh, I want to know Him. I want to know everything about Him! I *must* know Him! My Lord and my God!

He is the living Christ that creates within me the delight of His person, the joy of His spirit, and the peace of His heart. Jesus Christ—the same yesterday, today, and forever! I stand in awe and reverence of Him. He is holy, and He makes me holy before Him. Christ has become my life and my salvation.

Like Peter, all the sorrow is gone. Christ has triumphed, and I will not stand on the outside looking in anymore. I see Him clearly, for He washed my sins and sorrows away! In my weakness Jesus loved me and gave Himself for me. It happened to Peter. He wandered through the darkness and bitterness of his soul. But Jesus took it all away. The sorrow is gone. The doubts and fears have vanished!

Now Peter is stepping out of the shadows, Hallelujah! He is walking in the light of a risen Savior. The light of Christ is shining upon his face and in his heart. Peter knows the Lord now in a way he never knew Him before. Christ triumphed in him by bringing life and light to his heart and mind.

Peter became the first apostle to stand up for Jesus and proclaim the good news. On the day of Pentecost, Peter stood up. He was no longer running or hiding but now proclaiming Christ to a lost and dying world.

When we are set on fire with the word of Christ in our hearts and upon our lips, we too will come out of the shadows of fear and uncertainty and proclaim Him. And there will be no doubt that Jesus is alive in us. When the church wakes up and walks in the light of a living Christ, we will leave the darkness of self-gratification and serve Him in the spirit of truth.

When you and I are finished with our weeping, our sobbing and crying, and feeling sorry for ourselves, we will look up and see Jesus. He's watching over us, and He will shine the grace of God upon our hearts, and the glory of Christ's love will be manifested to us. The light has come, and the glory of a risen Savior is upon us.

The Lord is saying to us, "Your sins are forgiven. You are washed and made clean by the blood of the Lamb. Come out into the light of my grace and proclaim me to the world. Walk in the light, and be filled with my spirit, all that I am in you." When we begin to hear the Lord speaking to our hearts, there will be no question of the reality of God in this world.

Such men as this, like Peter, turned the world upside down for Christ. That's why we must tell others what we know. Praise God! Tell them! What God has made revealed needs to be proclaimed to the whole world.

As you tell others, you learn more of Jesus, and you grow nearer to Him. You know Him, and better still, He knows you. His word abides in you. You begin to see the Lord in every line, every verse, every chapter. He is written there. We can see Jesus when Moses spoke; it was about Him. When David spoke, it was Him. You can read Him in Isaiah and Daniel. Hallelujah! When the Holy Ghost speaks, it's Him—it's Jesus.

Best of all, the same Jesus that is there, is now in you! How do I know Jesus is my life? Because He's speaking in me!

Is Christ speaking in your heart? Is He telling you, "I Am?!" Do you know He lives in you? Are you ready to let the light of His word speak through you? "Let your light so shine before men," He said. Christ is worth knowing. Let us not be ashamed. Let us not hold back. Let us ever proclaim the good news of Jesus.

Christ is the seed of promise, the righteousness of Abraham, the Rock in the wilderness, the song of David and shepherd of my heart, the wisdom of the ages, the suffering servant, the root of Jesse, counselor and mighty God, everlasting Father and Prince of peace. He is the Savior of my soul. He is my soon coming King.

Let us walk in the light as He is in the light. We are no longer living in the shadows of fear and uncertainty, not struggling behind in the emptiness of our souls. We are the children of light and filled with light. We have the spirit of God and are not confused nor confounded, doubtful nor in despair.

Jesus Christ is alive *for* us. He is alive *in* us. He will never leave us and will always be there. Live and love in His name, brethren. And the world will know that "He is."

Father, I thank you because you have sent the living Christ into our hearts. Lift us up in your might and in your power. You have clothed us with your righteousness, and we are not ashamed but are thankful for all you've done for us in Christ. We know your will is being accomplished in this earth. And the enemy is not going to stop it. Grant us to proclaim your truth upon every housetop and tell the world of your love for them—that Jesus died and lives for them. Oh Father, you have called us to do so in the all-powerful name of Jesus.

Chapter 7

God Has Plans

God made all things, and everything He made has a place, a purpose. Everything has a reason for being, and that includes every one of us. God placed everything in order as it pleased His will. Everything was made to work as He wanted it. Then Satan came in and distorted and disrupted what God made.

So, this is the thought I want to share with you. When Jesus came it was to create a new order of things. The first order is decaying and passing away, but Jesus came to reveal that God would make all things new through Him. That's a beautiful thought. The first creation of God became defiled and fallen, but when the Lord sent Jesus, His plan was to recreate all things and set them in order in Christ.

That newness has given fallen man hope in Christ, enough hope for the whole world. Not only that, but Jesus has a plan to make each one of our lives new. He had those plans in mind before you and I were born. God's plan for man was something great. But when sin disrupted it, God already had a plan, plan B. It was already ready to put in place. God was ready no matter what Satan thought up or how hard he fought to destroy God's creation.

Your life and my life are not lost. God has a plan for you and a plan for me. He's had it all our lifetimes, and it's still unfolding every day. God called me into His ministry when I was a child, but His plan in my life keeps unfolding and revealing itself, the same way it is with all of us. God's not through with us until He decides He's through. I'm still here, so God still has more for me to do.

But I want to make this point very clear—God's purpose for us is in Christ.

Consider what happened to the apostle Peter. When Peter heard Jesus say that he would deny Him, Peter couldn't call Jesus a liar. Peter did deny saying, "No, I'll never do that." But Jesus did not rebuke Peter. He just simply told Peter what would happen. Jesus knew what would happen, no matter what Peter said. More than that, Jesus knew what would happen in Peter's life further down the road.

The Lord knows what the future holds of His people! Knowing that gives me a sense of confidence. It gives me a sense of rest and peace of mind. I know God has my future in His hands. The very next words Jesus says to Peter was, "Let not your heart be troubled."

Sometimes I wonder about my own life. I say, "Lord, you know I get perplexed and troubled and wonder about things." And the Lord says, "You worry and are troubled about too many things. You try to take too much on yourself. That's not your responsibility. That's not up to you; that's up to me. Just take one day at a time and walk close to me, and that's all you need to concern yourself with. I'll take care of the rest."

Then I can say, "My life is in your hands, Lord." You and I don't have to worry about our lives. We don't have to worry about what we're going to do the next day, week, or year. Just take one day at a time, knowing that you're in God's hands.

You'll also find that it's easier to listen to Christ as you draw close to Him. It becomes easier to love people, minister to people, and make Christ known. The closer you draw to Christ the easier it is for you to make Him known to the world. That's what's important.

Jesus told Peter and the rest, "Let not your hearts be troubled." Peter was probably thinking, "If I'm going to deny you, Lord, that's quite a mouthful. What you're saying *is* troubling me. I'm disturbed about this! I need some reassurance. Are you gonna leave me hanging?"

Jesus went on to say, "Don't let your hearts be troubled. You believe in God. Believe also in me." This is why I believe Jesus said that. The Jewish mind believed in God, Jehovah. They believed God made all things and that God was supreme. They had the law, the prophets, and they had the light that was given to the Jewish people. They knew the true God, and they were confident in that. Jesus was saying, "If you have confidence in God, the creator of all things, and if you believe God has called the Jews as a people unto Himself; if you believe all the prophets have said and written, then have confidence in me."

Then Jesus said something else. "In my Father's house there are many mansions." And then these words, "If it were not so, I would have told you" (John 14:2). The disciples didn't ask Him anything about His Father's house. So why did Jesus say, "If it were not so, I would have told you." I think He said that because He wants us to know we can rest assured that what Jesus wants us to know, He will tell us.

Sometimes we want to know more than what the Lord wants us to know. But we can take it easy, relax. We don't have to be so apprehensive and anxious. If the Lord wants us to know something, He'll tell us. And whatever it is, you can rest assured it's true.

Remember what Jesus said when the disciples asked Him to teach them to pray? He said, "Give us this day our daily bread." Whatever God wants you to have today, He will give it to you. Don't worry about tomorrow. God knows your past, and He knows your future. If He wants to tell you something about your future, He'll tell you.

Think about what Jesus told Peter. What He had to tell Peter was hard, upsetting. Don't you know Peter was hoping Jesus had something better to tell him? I don't know about you, but I don't want Jesus to tell me that the first thing I'm going to do is fail Him and deny Him! I want to know I'm going to be successful for the Lord and how good everything is going to be.

Peter had the same disappointed feeling. Can you imagine how he must have felt when the Lord told him that? But Jesus is the Lord, and He doesn't lie. Have you ever had something slap you in the face? And then the Lord says, "Don't be troubled." Man, how many times has it happened in my life. Things go wrong, and I say, "God, what's happening here? We're getting close to the edge. We're about to the end of our rope. Where are you?"

So, the Lord delivers this bad news, and just when the disciples are downcast, this happens in John 14:19. Jesus says, "Yet a little while and the world sees me not more. But you see me." Why did they see Jesus? The disciples were men just like everybody else, just like me and you. But Jesus revealed Himself to them. He called the disciples to follow and learn from Him. He called them to make Himself and His word known to them. This made the disciples witnesses of Jesus.

When Jesus called His disciples, He told them He was going to send them out to cast out devils, heal the sick, raise the dead, cleanse the lepers. They went across the land of Israel, preaching the gospel and healing the sick in all the cities and towns. We don't know how extensive this was, but for a time period in Jesus' ministry the disciples went out and preached the gospel.

The disciples came back to report to Jesus all the good things that happened. They were all excited and joyful. They were beside themselves rejoicing over what God had done. They said to Jesus, "Devils are subject unto us through your name." But what is the first thing Jesus said to them? He said, "I beheld Satan as lightning falls from heaven. Rejoice not because devils are subject unto you through my name, but rather rejoice because your name is written in heaven" (Luke 10:17).

Jesus Christ was speaking about what He knows of the future. He knows the plans He has for you. He called you by your name! Jesus calls and speaks things that be not as though they were. He said, "Your name is written in heaven." Even though they hadn't been redeemed, yet. The Holy Ghost hadn't come to them yet. But Jesus knew He called and ordained them, and declared, "They are mine. I know my sheep and my sheep know my voice and they will follow me" (John 10:27).

Jesus said to the disciples, "The world will see me, and after a little while no more." Oh, what a sorrowful sad thing! The world who rejected Christ—the great wonderful man who came and proclaimed the good news, healed the sick, raised the dead, cleansed the leper, made the blind see, the lame walk, the deaf to hear, and the dumb to speak. They rejected He who came with such power, grace, and showed forth His glory to the world. They will see Him no more.

Remember what Jesus said once to the people? "I am the light of the world," He said. "As long as I am in the world, I'm the light of the world. Walk in the light while you have it" (John 9:5). He was warning them that the time was coming when they won't have the light. It'll be gone. Even though they saw the light of Christ, they rejected Him anyway. And now the time was coming when, Jesus said, "They will see me no more."

But Jesus had a different message for the disciples. He said, "You see me. And because I live, you shall live also" (John 14:19). That's not the natural man that Jesus is talking about. He's talking about His new creation. When the Lord saved me and you, do you know what the Holy Ghost said? He said, "Let the real Bob Joyce stand up." Jesus isn't talking about raising up the old man that you were. He's talking about the new man you are in Christ. That's the man that's going to shake the world!

When Jesus said, "Let not your hearts be troubled." Who was He talking to? He was talking to the old man. He's talking to that natural man. He's talking to the man who's weighed down with problems and sin. He's talking to the man that's weighed down with doubts and fear.

But Jesus, speaking about what's to come, said, "I know you and what's going to happen to you. You don't have to be troubled about the things coming your way because I've got you in the palm of my hand. And nothing that's going to destroy you."

We may have to go through the fire for a minute. We're going to be tried as gold in the fire, but don't be afraid. Jesus knows the end from the beginning. He sees what's ahead. And you are going to make it. Why? Because it's not me getting myself through it, but it's me in Christ, hallelujah.

We can't lose. We're winning in Christ Jesus. As a matter of fact, we've already won. Whenever you have doubts about winning, that's Satan and the doubt of your own mind. But when you realize the truth in Jesus and the work God has done, you will realize you are a winner in Christ. It's not because of what you *do* for Him. It's because of who you *are* in Him.

Jesus works out your life. He works out your future. He works out what you're going to accomplish and what you won't accomplish. That's true for you and me. I just want to learn to leave it all in His hands. I want to say, "Lord, I believe this is what you've called me to do. If this is what you want me to do, then I know you'll make a way. God, I don't know how I'm going do it, but you know how you're going to do it. Lord, I don't know what's happening to me next, but you do. My life is in your hands. Everything about me is in your hands. My economy is in your hands. My family is in your hands."

Oh, the new things God will make in Christ Jesus. "Behold, I will work a work in your days," God told the Jews through the prophets. "You will wonder and perish, it will all be declared unto you. But behold, I will make a new work" (Acts 13:41). What's that new work? It's a renewal, a recreation in Christ Jesus. Adam's race has fallen. But Christ's race has risen, hallelujah.

71

Jesus said in my Father's house are many mansions. The word *mansion* means dwelling place. Now there's something here that's beautiful. God dwells in the humble heart and meek spirit. When God created all things, in the beginning, He had a place for everything in the natural physical world. But Jesus said now I go away to prepare a place for you, a dwelling place. What dwelling place has Christ prepared that He's created for me and you? It's in Him.

We are going to go to heaven. That's part of it. Yes, it's a physical tangible place, but it's also a spiritual place. Jesus said, "Behold I prepare a place for you that where I am, you may be also" (John 14:3). Where is He? He's seated at the right hand of power. He's ascended into heaven far above all principalities and powers, and all powers in heaven and earth are subject to Him. Jesus is right there seated at the right hand of the Father, and He says, "Where I am, that's where you're going to be."

So, what has God created? What is the purpose of our lives? What is the purpose of Jesus' coming? What is the reason for His death, burial, and resurrection? He did all that so we may be seated with Him in heavenly places. It's not the same as it is on earth. This dwelling place that Jesus is talking about is not from Adam's race or anything you see in the physical world. It's in a *spiritual* place, where we will sit with Christ. Think about that.

In order not to confuse anyone, I should emphasize that I believe Heaven is a real place, physical and tangible. I believe in the pearly gates, streets made of gold. I believe there are walls made of jasper and all sorts of diamonds and gems. It's tangible, but it's also spiritual. There's a tree of life, and I'll be eating the fruit of that tree. I believe if I died and went to heaven today, the Lord would allow me to see that river of life flowing from the throne of God.

But I want to tell you that even though we can't partake of the physical right now, we can partake of the spiritual! Right here on earth we are offered the same spiritual fruit, the same spiritual tree, and the same spiritual water. And heavenly places are right now in your spirit. Jesus created it in you.

Why do I know I'm going to heaven? Why am I so sure that I'm going to a tangible place called heaven? Because Jesus purchased my passage at the cross, and He's already placed me there. Maybe that sounds crazy to you. But it sounds crazy because you don't see in the spiritual world. If you saw in the spiritual world, you would understand. I'm in that heavenly place in Christ right now, and I'm eating and drinking of His life and rejoicing in His glory. I see it! I don't see all, but I see it in part.

So now, Jesus calls those things that be not as though they were. That means that I'm saved by faith. By grace are ye saved through faith, that not of yourselves it is a gift of God. We're already saved.

The Bible says when the Lord comes and takes us out of here, our bodies will be changed into a glorified body, which is a spiritual body. It's just like heaven. It's tangible—you can feel it. It eats, drinks, feels, and touches. But do you know what else it can do? It can walk through walls and disappear and reappear. Maybe it can take off flying. I don't know. But everything that we can do now in this physical fleshly body will still be there, and more. But there will no longer be decay and pain and sin.

We've entered into that heavenly place that's prepared for us. Jesus said, "I go away to prepare a place for you that where I am there you will be also." He said, "Because I live you will live." He's calling out you and me, just like Peter. But Jesus isn't calling out the dead man. He's calling out the *new* man. He's calling out the new creation that God makes in Christ Jesus.

When you're walking along in life, don't worry about tomorrow. When you walk out in the world today, consider yourself walking in heavenly places. I know I'm still here, Lord, but at the same time, I'm not here because I'm with you!

The Lord said to Peter, "It's alright, Peter. I see what's going to happen to you. I know your life, and I know who you are. I know what you're made out of. You think you're so strong, but you're really weak. You think you're a bold one, but you're a coward. But that's alright. That's alright."

We come to the Lord and say, "God, I'm not worth anything. I want to do right, but I'm weak." The Lord says, "I know your heart. I know what's in your life. I know what's in your spirit. I know what's on your mind. You can't fool me because I know all about you. Don't let your heart be troubled. Don't be troubled about that."

That's the hope God gives every one of us in Christ every day. He knows we take our eyes off of Jesus and put them on everything else. He knows the old self and our old ways, and He knows how the old flesh wants to rule your life. The Lord knows what's going to happen before you do it. "But," He says, "there's a place beside me that I made for you, and this is where I want you to be."

I want to do great and mighty works for God. I want to serve Him with all my heart. But all the Lord wants from me is to stay right in the place He prepared for me beside Him. Because when we're there with Him, all those hopes, dreams, and desires come out of us through Him. He fulfills in our lives what He has planned for us because we found our place in Him.

How do we get people excited about the Lord? We do that by getting stirred up ourselves. We don't have to be concerned about everybody else and what they think because when we get excited, suddenly everybody starts getting excited. You'll wonder how that happened. And people will tell you they saw you get so happy in the Lord that wanted it, too. They saw you rejoicing in the Lord, crying, singing, or shouting, and then the Lord gets ahold of their hearts and then they start praising God, too.

Don't let your hearts be troubled. I'm going to prepare a place for you that where I am, you may be also. Are we with Jesus now? Is He with us now? He didn't say where I'm *going* to be. He said, where I *am* there will you be also. In Christ's mind, He's already there. When Jesus said these words, He hadn't shed His blood, yet. But in the mind of Jesus, it was already done. He hadn't died or risen, but Jesus saw it as done.

In the same way, we are already in Heaven with Jesus. It just hasn't been manifested, yet. We haven't seen Jesus face to face, and even still, He's with us.

He said, "If I go and prepare a place for you, I will come again and receive you to myself that where I am there you may be also." Every one of us who is born again is yearning to be with Jesus. We're yearning to see Him. What we're feeling is a grand love for Him. God knows you love Him. God knows you want to see Him.

There are people we love to be around for one reason or another. Maybe they encourage us, make us laugh, or they're just likable. You can't help but like them. That's the way it is with us and Jesus. We pray, "I want to see you, Lord. I want to be next to you. I want to see what you look like." Don't you wonder if Jesus' hair is brown or white or whatever? I wonder about things like that, and I want to know. We adore Him! We worship every inch of Him. You don't have to worship the ground He walks on because He *made* the ground you walk on.

But I'm not discouraged that I have to wait to see Him because Jesus has given me His promise and, even better, His spirit. And He has given me a place beside Him. What a privilege it is to walk with God, to hear His words and to trust Him. He speaks to our hearts in the most solemn and tender way. You might not hear His voice like human sounds, but you hear it just the same. It's just as real, just as good, and it's more beautiful than any voice as He whispers to your spirit, "Be not troubled. I am with you. Don't be upset about your problem. Don't be upset about your failure. I go to prepare a place for you. You have a place beside me. Don't wander off, son. Don't let the enemy attract your mind away from me. Let your mind be stayed on me. Think of the truths I give you. They will transform you."

Your heart is being transformed by the renewing of your mind, so the real you that God's created for Himself will come out. God doesn't want to clothe you in *your* righteousness. He wants to clothe you with the righteousness of Christ. We're walking in that spiritual place with Jesus right now because He said we are.

Even though we don't see Him with our eyes right now, one day we will. He's going to reveal Himself and how blessed we're going to be. Jesus will finally manifest Himself to the world and let them behold all His glory. But, until then my heart will go on singing, hallelujah. Until then with joy I'll carry on. Until the day my eyes behold that city. Until the day He calls me home. I won't see Him with my physical eyes, but my heart will go on singing.

What gives me a reason to keep singing? Jesus put me in that spiritual place with Him, and one day the real tangible place will manifest itself. On that day, I'm going to walk and talk with the angels because Jesus said I will. Only Jesus has enough power to make that happen. That's the place Jesus went to prepare.

Quit thinking about mansions. I don't want a mansion; I want Jesus. Don't think about the golden streets. I don't care about walking on golden streets. I want to walk with Jesus. I'd rather walk with Him beside an old creek somewhere than on golden streets. It doesn't matter, as long as I'm with Jesus.

But I'm telling you, we don't have to wait till we get to heaven to walk with Jesus. That's the way it is right now. We're walking with Jesus in a dirty darkened world. We're walking in a world that is degraded and fallen down, a world that Satan has destroyed and corrupted, polluted with wickedness, and ungodliness reigns everywhere. But we're walking with Jesus.

Christ was here on this earth when things were corrupt, even as they are now, but He was the light of the world. He said, "I prepare a place for you. The world will see me no more, but you will." Do you see Him? "Because I live," He said, "you will live."

Jesus called you out of the darkness and traditions of men. He called you out of ignorance, darkness, and misunderstanding into His marvelous light. Now we know Christ in spirit. Now we see Him in the spirit for what He truly is. Now we understand.

It was a wonder for the disciples to walk with a man that could raise the dead and walk on water, but through the Holy Ghost, we now know who God truly is. We understand. Jesus is so glorious, more glorious now than He was when He was here. Jesus said, "He that believeth on the works that I do shall he do also and greater works than these shall he do because I go to the Father" (John 14:12).

And the greater works are happening all around us. The spiritually dead are being raised up all over the world. People are coming to Christ everywhere. They're coming out of their dead sin and unto life eternal. Forget raising the physically dead. That doesn't save anybody. God can raise the dead. He can heal the sick, and open the eyes of the blind. I've seen Him do things like that in my own life. But that don't save anybody. They go off their own way forget about the Lord.

What's really exciting is when Jesus gets ahold of a life, and He won't let go. Oh Lord, don't ever let me go! Don't ever let me get out of this place. I want to be with you.

Doesn't it make you feel like telling somebody? Don't you feel like shouting to the top of your lungs? Do you feel like getting on the house top and telling the world? Man, I tell you, when the church gets on fire like that, look out world, look out devil, look out! We're coming!

I thank you, Father. I praise you. That's all I know to do. Here I am. Fill me overflowing with your spirit. Let the Holy Spirit come and refresh me. Make me new, Lord. That's what I want. I want to be with you, in your presence. Every day on this earth with you is better than the day before in Christ Jesus, amen.

Chapter 8

Take Heed What You Hear

Jesus referred to the kingdom of God time and again. He likened it unto many things. He likened the kingdom of God to things like a great net that was cast into the sea and gathered many fish. And when they brought them to shore, they separated the good from the bad.

Jesus said the kingdom of Heaven is likened unto a woman who took three measures of meal and hid leaven in the meal until the whole was leaven. Leaven is yeast, and when you put yeast in the flour it permeates the whole lump. That's the way the kingdom of God is.

You know we hear a lot lately about what's going on in the world, especially Washington. The news is constant, and when I consider everything that's happening with my flesh and my reasoning, I get angry. I see certain people who think they are getting an advantage in our country. There are men who manipulate and create their desired outcomes to happen. They manipulate the economy and other parts of the system.

They act like they want to create a utopian world, but here's the fly in the buttermilk. The kingdom they want to create, if they get their way, won't last very long. Whatever man contrives, whatever he thinks he can accomplish, whatever goal he may set, or however many people he brings under control, it's all going to come tumbling down around his ears. Because the kingdom of God shall stand, and all the other kingdoms of the earth will be crushed to powder.

Remember the vision of Daniel? He saw the stone and mountain cut without hands hit the image at his feet (Daniel 2:34). All those kingdoms were destroyed, and they were like the shaft on the threshing floor as the wind blew it away. All the kingdoms of this world are going to come down. Christ is going to rule forevermore.

But here's what I want to tell you today. Christ's kingdom is now. His kingdom is right now in the hearts of every believer.

Jesus said that the kingdom of God was like a man who planted grain, and he let it grow (Matthew 13:24-30). But while the workers slept, the enemy came in and sowed tares among the wheat. When the men woke up the next morning, they came to the Lord and said, "Lord, did you not plant wheat? Where then did the tares come from?" And the Lord said, "An enemy's done this." They asked, "Shall we pluck up the tares and burn them?" The Lord said, "No, not yet, lest ye pluck up the wheat with it. Let them grow together until the time of harvest. Then gather up those tares in bundles to burn. But gather my wheat and put them in the barns."

Jesus later explained to His disciples what it meant. He said, "The enemy is the devil that sowed those tares." What Jesus said here takes me back to Genesis. Remember when Satan came in the form of a serpent and spoke to the woman. What was he doing? He was sowing his lies. Jesus said for us to take heed what we hear because what we hear is what's going to be in our hearts. It will take root and form fruit that comes forth out of the mouth. Everything that's bottled up inside is going to come out. Whatever is in our hearts and minds is what we say.

So, Satan is the one that planted the seeds of lies and falsehood. And what did it bring forth? It made every man stand guilty. But when we hear the words of Jesus, it sows the seed of the Son of Man. And just like in the beginning, when God created the trees, He said, "Let the fruit bearing trees, whose seed is in itself, come forth" (Genesis 1:11).

Everything that God created had the seed in itself, so it could bring forth creation of its own kind. What came first the chicken or the egg? The chicken! But the chicken didn't come empty handed. He came with an egg on the inside, so that the chicken could bring forth of its kind. God created the animals and plants to have seeds and to come forth after their kind.

The old devil came along, and he got the idea from the Lord to plant a seed. But he perverts the word of the Lord, and Satan brings falsehood and casts doubt on the word of God. By doing that, he raises up men who also cast doubt. When men fall into the lies of Satan, they sow the tares of doubt. So, the seeds of God's truth and the tares of Satan's lies grow at the same time.

Satan, he's a sly old fox. He's been everywhere, busy planting lies all these years. But, you know, God's been busy, too. Through it all, God is still growing seeds somewhere. Somebody somewhere always has an ear to hear, and God is raising them up. Jesus said, "He that has ears to hear, let him hear."

So, the word of God tells us, "Take heed what you hear," because there's two voices out there, two "words," if you will. One is true, and one is false. One comes from God and the other comes from Satan. There's nothing in between, only right and wrong, good and evil.

Let me read you the words of Jesus in Luke 8:16-18, "No man, when he hath lighted a candle, covereth it with a vessel, or putteth it under a bed; but setteth it on a candlestick, that they which enter in may see the light. For nothing is secret, that shall not be made manifest; neither anything hid, that shall not be known and come abroad. Take heed therefore how ye hear: for whosoever hath, to him shall be given; and whosoever hath not, from him shall be taken even that which he seemeth to have."

Jesus says no man lights a candle and then covers it with a vessel or puts it under a bed, and that's exactly what Satan tries to do with the word of God. He tries to hide it with a lie. That's what Satan did to Eve. Satan perverts what God says and tries to make his own story appear to be right. Essentially, he's calling God a liar.

Satan basically told Eve, "You can do this. You can. Go ahead and eat the tree. It won't bother you. It won't kill you. It's alright. You'll become wise. As a matter of fact, you'll be like God." Satan called God a liar in the beginning, and it's been that way ever since.

You see, words are so important. What we hear is important. What we allow to come into our hearts through hearing is so important because it's going to determine what and who we are and how we live, think, and act. What we listen to not only affects loving one another here and now, but it also has to do with our eternal souls.

So, words are so important. What we receive into our spirits becomes a part of who we are, so we need to make sure we know the truth. That's why Jesus warns us to take heed to what we hear. He said, "He that has ears to hear let him hear."

Jesus goes on to say when a man lights a candle, he doesn't cover it with a vessel or put it under a bed, but he sits it on a candlestick that they which enter in may see the light. God's word is not meant to be hidden; it's meant to be heard. It is the light that drives away the darkness. It brings life and liberty to all those who believe. But only those who hear God's word can receive it.

Then listen to what Jesus said. "Nothing is secret that shall not be made manifest, neither anything hid that shall not be known and come abroad." Whatever a man has within him will come abroad. This means, whatever a man thinks will come about. People will know a person by what he thinks. They'll know what he believes by what's in inside of him. People will see his actions and hear his words. There's nothing hidden.

If you're a blind man walking down the street, everybody's going to know you're blind. If you're an ignorant man, people are going to know that. Every time you say something, it reveals part of what and who you are. There isn't anything hidden that won't be seen.

Some folks think they can hide what they are, but sooner or later it comes out in the open, and everyone knows. The way the people talk today, it's the result of what they've been hearing. The teachings of the schools and colleges are soaking down into their spirits through their minds. Oldtimers used to talk about the religion of Grandma. Whatever Grandma said was right, and that's what people believed. But suppose Grandma was wrong? Let's be sure what we listen to is God's word. That's how we guarantee we have light inside of us, not darkness.

Jesus said that men have light, but the light that is in them is darkness. Men have knowledge, but it's not the wisdom of God. Therefore, their knowledge is worthless. It's all perishing. If the light in you is darkness, how great is the darkness!

All the time our spirits are being fed with what we're hearing and seeing. So then what should we be feeding on? Those of us who are born again, we are born of the word, which is the eternal living word of God. Then it is by that word that we must be nourished. It is by that word that we must live. I can't get the nourishment I need by hearing anything else. Nothing will strengthen me but the pure unadulterated word of God.

That's the same with us as natural human beings. What are we born of? Naturally speaking, we're born of this earth. God told Adam, "Dust thou art and from dust thou shalt return" (Genesis 3:19). That's why we say, "Ashes to ashes, dust to dust" at funerals. We're all born of the dust. So where do we get our nourishment? The dust. We get all our vegetables from the ground. All the nutrients, vitamins, and minerals can be found in rocks. We eat animals, but where do the animals get their food from? The ground. So, man is nourished physically by that which he was born from. He must have it, or he will die.

We are the same way spiritually. The spirit must have nourishment by the spirit, and our food is the word of God. We can't make it without God's word. We must hear it, understand it, and meditate on it. We have to be filled with it.

The Bible said this seed then will bring forth fruit of its kind. So, as we take in God's word, the seed is planted, and finally brings forth its own kind. We are the fruit of God's love. We're walking around because we have Jesus on the inside, His word in our heart, His word in our spirit, and the word of life in Christ shines through us.

This light can't be hidden. You can't put it under a bushel. You can't stop it or set it aside. If the life of Christ is in you, it has to be seen. If Christ is in your heart, He's going to come out of your mouth.

Somebody said, "I'm afraid to tell somebody that I'm saved and know the Lord." I don't think that person is saved at all. You see, if the Lord is present in their spirit, it will come forth. Either a tree is good or it's bad. There is no in-between. Either a person has the life of Christ, or that person is dead. Jesus said by the fruit you will know them. A good tree brings forth good fruit; an evil tree brings forth evil fruit.

And then Jesus said, take heed to what you hear. Why did He say that? Because there isn't anything hidden that will not be made known. If you go around listening to the devil, you're going to talk like the devil. Isn't that right? If you read, watch, and think on evil things, then that's all you're going to talk about. If you read and believe falsehood, then all your talk will be falsehood.

Did you know that lies and deceptions don't do anything for you but rob your life? It doesn't add anything; it only takes away. Living a lie doesn't make everything comfortable and right. It doesn't satisfy. But the truth satisfies. The truth enlightens. The truth brings light and joy and peace.

As a result, a man can come boldly to God. You see, God doesn't want us to seek Him, cowering down behind a rock. God doesn't want man to be buried in the darkness of his mind. When God saves a man,

He brings him out of the humiliation of his own darkness, and God brings him boldly into His presence.

God has not called us to be afraid of Him. God called us to come boldly. We can walk right up to Him and call Him "Father." That's what light and truth do—they take away our shame, so we can walk in boldness. It's the kind of boldness that gives us the ability to stand up in the face of great adversity and proclaim truth. Not because I said it or you said it, but because God said it. If we would learn to take our stand upon the solid rock, when the enemy comes in like a flood, the Lord will raise up a standard against him.

We need to learn to rejoice in what the Lord says. If we're happy in what God says, the truth will shine forth to everyone around. We don't have to cower down to people around us, trying to hide who we are, but we can come boldly declaring what lives inside us. It's not our own righteousness that makes us bold, but it's Jesus Christ in our hearts.

When Jesus walked on earth, He didn't cower down and hide behind walls. No, brother, He stood up on the mountain and shouted out so everyone could listen to Him. He said, "Draw that boat over to me. So many people are around me, I don't have room here on the shore. Bring that boat over here so I can stand in it and preach to these people." So, they brought the boat for Him.

Jesus didn't let anything stop Him from speaking the truth. He didn't let the enemy make Him fearful. He didn't allow the Pharisees or priests in the temple to quiet Him down. If anything, Jesus' enemies emboldened Him.

Jesus was the light, and the light blinded them because they were in darkness. Jesus came to give light, and God called us to share that light with the world. We are to boldly proclaim what we know to be true.

When God saved us, it wasn't some little something done in the corner. Something exploded down in your soul. It was the greatest thing that's ever happened in your life. You might have wished you'd known Jesus years before. You never knew the peace and joy you now know in Him. And people see a change in you. When God reveals Himself to man, He doesn't do it behind closed doors. He proclaims Himself through man's spirit.

God makes Himself known to us through the spirit by His word. He proclaims Himself boldly, so in return we stand upright and proclaim the word without shame. We sing songs and praises out loud. We shout! We're not ashamed to call His name. We're not ashamed to tell the world what Jesus has done for us and what He can do for them.

What God does the whole world sees. Satan's the one that likes to creep in behind closed doors. He doesn't want people to know what he's doing. He's the one that brings blinders and deception to the world, causing men to sneak around and slither in dark places.

But God proclaims the light, and you and I are children of that light. Therefore, our lives are made to proclaim His glory. That's how Jesus was, and that's the way we need to be.

Sometimes our flesh gets in the way, and we want to keep our mouth shut, but God help us to open our mouths and speak what the world needs to hear.

Jesus tells us to take heed what we hear. Christians, if you listen to something other than the Lord, His life-giving light won't be seen as much. Turn your eyes toward Christ, and you see His love and grace to you in all its fullness. God, help me to be that. Help me to let Christ live fully in me.

Paul said, "It's not me that lives but Christ that lives in me" (Galatians 2:20). He said, "I'm pressing on that I may apprehend that for which I am also apprehended of Christ" (Philippians 3:12). What are we apprehended for? Jesus didn't save us so we would sit over in the corner. He apprehended me for a reason.

The Lord wants to turn us loose. He wants that fire to burn within us and fuel us to do more. God, forgive me if I ever try to put water on it. Burn in me, Lord. I don't want to water you down. Lord, blow on the embers in my heart. Blow on that little flame so it gets hotter and bigger.

The Holy Spirit is always there, bringing us into fellowship. He's always speaking, driving us, and drawing us to Himself. Remember who you are and what you have in Christ. The treasure you have is great. Don't hide it. Don't put it in a closet or under a bushel. Let the world see the light that's in you.

Take heed. The only way that happens is to hear what the Spirit is saying. And what is the Spirit saying? He's always speaking the words of Christ to our hearts. Let's get our minds and hearts into the word of God so it penetrates every fiber of our beings. It's like being a sponge. A sponge gets so full of water, when you squeeze it, nothing but water comes out. If you soak up the Spirit, when someone squeezes you, only the love of God is going to come out. You'll be overflowing with the life-giving love of God.

Take heed what you hear. Our witness depends on it. Jesus said, "I didn't come in my own name, but I came in my Father's." He said, I don't speak my own words, but I speak the words of the Father that sent me" (John 5:43). The scripture says, "And those whom God sent speak the words of God" (John 3:34). If we're born of the word, let us speak the word of God. Let us saturate our lives, our spirits, our minds in the word of God.

Jesus was perfect, and His perfection is in us. We're not perfect ourselves, but He is. If we let Christ speak in us, our words and actions will be perfect. Let the world see the perfection of Jesus in us. Then our lives will be full. Life is not complicated any more. It takes away the burdens of the world. That's our destiny.

Father, I thank you for your word that lives and abides forever. I pray, Lord, that you help each one of us. Help us pay attention to what we let our minds dwell on. While we're running around living life here and there, help us to stop and take heed to what we hear from you. We want our lives to be full of you. In Jesus' name, amen.

Chapter 9

Testimony of God

The Ten Commandments were written by God on stone tablets. God gave them to Moses to declare a testimony of God's law. The law testifies to our sin, and God's testimony to man was that we are guilty before Him.

God's precepts are holy, just, and perfect. The Bible says they are perfect concerning the soul. God's law is perfect, and it testifies against man's imperfections. The law can't eradicate sin. It can only show what sin is. It can't give life. It can only bring death because everyone falls short of keeping God's Law.

Moses put God's holy law in the holiest place—within the Ark of the Covenant. But God put something else in His holy place. He commanded Moses to include a mercy seat, a lid on top of this Ark. God said to Moses, "I want you to put the mercy seat over the Ark of the Testimony" (Exodus 25:21). You see, the mercy seat is above that testimony.

God's law had been broken, but He prepared a place of mercy. And instead of putting the law above mercy, He placed mercy over the law. Isaiah 8:13 says, "Sanctify the Lord of Host Himself and let Him be your fear and let Him be your dread, and He shall be for a sanctuary, but for a stone of stumbling and for a rock of offence, to both the houses of Israel for a gin and a snare for the inhabitance of Jerusalem."

Paul quotes this scripture in the book of Romans, where he speaks of Christ, the rock of offence and a stone of stumbling. He said, "The builders of the temple stumbled over that stumbling stone" (Romans 9:30-33). When the Jews built their temple, they had all these stones cut, brought in, and laid around. The master builder chose the stones. They had to be the perfect cut. And the corner stone had to be blemish free. It had to be absolutely perfectly square, so that all the other stones that were put in place would fit right up against this stone to keep everything in line.

The Bible says Jesus was the cornerstone that was rejected. The Jews said, "No, this stone doesn't fit into our plans." So, they rejected it. The perfect stone was lying there, and they went right by it. Not only that, they stumbled over it and fell on the ground. The Bible says, "Behold I lay in Zion a foundation of stone, and he that believes on Him shall not be ashamed" (Isaiah 28:16).

Now, the next verse says to bind up the testimony. This is the seal of the law among His disciples. God's making changes here. He's doing something wondrous. He's saying, "I'm going to show those that believe in me things they've never heard. They're going to have mysteries revealed to them that have been kept secret from the beginning of the world."

God is going to bind up the testimony, but He will seal the law in the hearts of His people. The Bible says that we are sealed by the Holy Spirit until the day of redemption. So that everything God placed within us is sealed. The binding of the testimony means to seal it up, put it away. It loses its power.

Reading on, the word says, "I will wait upon the Lord. Then he hides his face from the house of Jacob. I will look for him, behold, I am the children whom the Lord has given to me" (Isaiah 8:17). Hebrews says the same thing, quoting Isaiah, "Behold I am the children whom the Lord has given to me. For signs and wonders of Israel for the Lord of hosts which dwells in Mount Zion" (Hebrews 2:13).

When Christ came, He sealed the law among His disciples. But why did Jesus put away the old law. Is the law of God unjust? Is it unholy? No! The law of God is spiritual, holy, and good. But because man's flesh is weak, the law became weak because of the sinful flesh of man. It could not accomplish in man what God wanted to accomplish because man's flesh is weak and sinful.

But then Jesus came, and He wasn't weak like the law. He did what only God could do! "Thanks be unto God through Christ Jesus our Lord, behold therefore there is now no condemnation to them which are in Christ Jesus who walked not after the flesh but after the spirit.

For the law of the spirit of life in Christ Jesus has made me free from the law of sin and death" (Romans 8:1-2).

Talk about the testimony of life—Jesus Christ *is* the testimony of life. The law was given by Moses, but grace and truth came by Jesus. He said, "This is the new covenant that I will make with them in those days saith the Lord. Not like the fathers that brought them that took them by the hand and brought them out of the land of Egypt, but he said, this is a new covenant" (Hebrews 8:10).

God no longer relied on the nature of man to do what was right. Now, He puts the law in our hearts, within our very nature. He's going to write His laws in your mind, and He said, "Their sins will I remember no more" (Hebrews 10:17).

Let me give you just one example of this from the book of Psalms, which is so rich in the mercy of God. The spirit of the Lord was upon David, so his heart was after God. So, throughout the book of Psalms, David speaks by the spirit of the Lord and emphasizes His mercy.

Look at Psalms 85:7, "Show us thy mercy, Oh Lord, and grant us thy salvation. I will hear what God the Lord will speak for He will speak peace unto His people and to His saints, but let them not turn again to folly. Surely His salvation is nigh them that fear Him that glory may dwell in our land. Mercy and truth are met together. Righteousness and peace have kissed, fruit shall spring out of the earth, and righteousness shall look down from heaven. The Lord shall give that which is good, and our land shall increase. Righteousness shall go before him and shall set us in the way of his steps."

Let me read to you another beautiful verse in Psalms. This really sums up everything I want to bring to you. I pray the Holy Spirit makes it real to your hearts and minds. "Justice and judgement are the habitation of God's throne. There is none holy but thee, Oh God. Thou art the same, and your years never fail" (Psalm 89:14). There is no shadow of turning in God. He is the same. He is right and good. There's no one else that is beside Him. He is the eternal. He is God forevermore. This is what David is saying here.

Remember one time when a rich man came to Jesus and said, "Good master, what must I do to inherit eternal life?" (Luke 18:18-30). The first thing Jesus said was, "Why do you call me good? Only God's good." There's a hidden message right there. What was Jesus saying?

First of all, we know when Jesus came, He didn't come to speak of Himself, but He came to glorify the Father. He didn't brag on Himself.

He said, "Whatever I say is what the Father says, and I don't say anything He doesn't say" (John 12:49).

Only God is good. That rich man might not have seen who Jesus was, but we do. The rich man may have just seen a good teacher or miracle worker. If the rich man only knew he was speaking to God in the flesh. The rich man didn't know, but we know.

Jesus said the Father testifies of me. He says, "In your law it is written that everything shall be established by the word of two witnesses." He says, "I'm one and my Father is the other one that testifies of me. And I know that his testimony is true" (John 8:17-18).

Can God lie? No! When Jesus went down to be baptized by John what happened? When Jesus came up out of the water, the Spirit descended like a dove upon Him, and a voice from heaven said, "This is my beloved son in whom I'm well pleased. He testifies of me" (Matthew 3:17).

When God looks at us in Christ, He says the same thing. "You're my beloved children. With you, I'm well pleased." That's not the testimony Moses received from the mountain. That is the testimony Jesus received at the River Jordan. It's a testimony of life, not death.

Jesus came for our sakes. He came and said, "Behold thy brother which God has given me and the children that He's given to me" (Hebrews 2:13). God is pleased with Christ in all that He is, all that He did. Everything that is Christ's is imputed to us.

You're not perfect in yourself, but in Christ you are. Quit looking at yourself and start looking at yourself through Him. When God looks at us, He sees the testimony of Christ. In His eyes you are perfect, and He says, "I am pleased with you."

How is this possible? The word says, "He that believes in his heart and confesses with his mouth the Lord Jesus Christ, shall be saved" (Romans 10:9). It's faith.

But God doesn't just dismiss our sin. If He did that, He wouldn't be just. So, the debt had to be paid. Sin must be judged, and everything man does must be paid for in full. God is holy; therefore, no sin can enter His presence. That's what Jesus came for, to pay the debt. And we put our faith in the work of Christ.

Back to the Ark of the Covenant, that's where God met with His people, the Jews. And the law was God's testimony against us. But nothing evil can dwell in His presence. So, God said, "Moses, I want you to put the mercy seat over my testimony." Moses didn't know what God was doing, but those of us in the New Testament church, we know what He did.

The law was given by Moses, but grace and truth came by Jesus Christ. The word says, "Mercy and truth shall go before His face" (Psalm 89:14).

You see, everything is subservient to God. We can't even stand to look upon His face or we'd die. When God descended upon the mountain of Sinai, it shook. Man, that whole mountain just trembled. God put on a display of His might. All He had to do was put one foot on that mountain and the whole thing began to quake.

Even Moses started shaking. Moses knew that no man can stand before God, if He doesn't want you to. Only God can give a person the strength to stand before Him. God called Moses up the mountain. The Bible says Moses talked with the Lord, but this was only possible as God revealed Himself in such a way that Moses could stand it. Moses didn't see all of God's glory. Moses asked to see it, but God told him, no man can see my glory and live.

God's glory cannot be contained, not by men, not by all of creation. God asked Solomon about building a temple, and Solomon said, "I know you're the God of heaven and earth. And I know neither Heaven, earth, nor all the universe could contain you" (1 Kings 8:27). But the Lord said, "Go ahead and build it. But no one could enter God's presence without blood because a man's sin has to be paid for."

God doesn't want us to be afraid of Him, but we can't come to Him any other way. There's only one way to come to Him—the testimony of Christ. It's mercy and truth that have gone before the face of God. The Bible says when we look upon Christ, He is the express image of God, and His testimony is this: "Mercy and truth are met together; righteousness and peace have kissed each other" (Psalm 85:10).

Who is righteousness? God is righteous. But it says here that righteousness and peace have kissed each other. What does that mean? That means that Christ, who is our peace, has satisfied and pleased righteousness with all He did on the cross through love.

What is the greatest act of love? When Jesus stretched out His arms at the cross and said, "It's finished" (John 19:30). He died for us. Peace was made between God and mankind. We were redeemed, purchased through the blood of Christ.

So, Jesus becomes our peace. Let the mercy seat be over the testimony. David said, "By the spirit of God, Lord, thy desireth truth on the inward parts." He said, "Lord you know my heart. You know my ways. Forgive me of all my sin, even sins that I don't know of. Father, cleanse me, and I shall be clean. Wash me, and I shall be made whiter than snow. This is what delights God" (Psalm 51:6-9).

So mercy and truth have come together and goes before God's face. Peace and righteousness have kissed each other. And God, instead of coming in His blazing glory, He comes to us in the gentle and meekness of the spirit of His son. With arms stretched out He says, "Come unto me, and I will give you rest. Come unto me all ye that labor and are heavy laden" (Matthew 11:28). We were under the burden of the law, guilty under God's testimony, but Jesus said, "I'll redeem you, so you might live with God in righteousness and peace."

Christ came and cleared the way to God. He said, "I am the way." Jesus removed all the sin and guilt that separated us from God. In John 1:19-23, John the Baptist was not yet cast into prison. They came to him and said, "Tell us. Are you the Christ that should come?" He said, "No, I'm not. I'm the voice of one crying in the wilderness. I've come to prepare the way of the Lord. But what I am and what I do has been given to me."

John is explaining that he's happy to be what he is. He's not the Messiah, and he's glad he's not, because he represented the Messiah that is to come. That was a privilege for John. We should all be so glad to be what we are in Christ.

When I was a kid, I got saved and started preaching. I dreamed of being a great big tent preacher like A. A. Alan. But that was so foolish—a child's way of thinking. I didn't realize then that I could be happy to be what I already am. How many ten-year-old kids do you see preaching? I didn't realize how special that was at the time.

Now I'm all grown up, and no one special, just a preacher. But as I look back over my life, I realize how much God really has blessed me. Being called to preach at 10 years old is a wonderful thing. I'm glad I'm not A. A. Alan. I'm glad I'm Bob Joyce. If God wants to give me a big tent to preach in, bring it on. Otherwise, I'm glad to be right here where I'm at.

And that's what John's saying here. He's telling us to learn how to be content with what God's given us now. Then God will increase you, and your ministry will grow. He'll do things in your life you never dreamed that He would do through you. Let the Lord take care of your life, and He'll have the goals set for you. Whatever the Lord tells us to do, that's what we'll do.

Now, if you have an all-consuming burning desire to do something, that may be God dealing with you. Step out by faith. Maybe you're worried that you don't have any money. God says, "I own all the gold and silver. I own the cattle on a thousand hills" (Psalm 50:10).

Read what the word says in John 3:28-29, "Ye yourselves bear me witness that I said I am not the Christ but that I was sent before Him. He that has the bride is the bridegroom, but the friend of the bridegroom (which is what John was) which stands and hears Him, rejoices greatly because of His voice. Thus, my joy, therefore, is fulfilled."

John lived in the wilderness, eating locust and wild honey. He wore nothing but rags all his life—camel hair and skins. He didn't live delicately by any means. John didn't have a home, nowhere to lay his head at night. He slept by the creeks and ate out of the trees, whatever God gave him. He had all he needed because he knew who he belonged to and who sent him.

And John was content to be who he was because he knew the Messiah had finally come. John said, "He must, therefore, increase and I must decrease" (John 3:30). Why? Because the Lord does not give the spirit by measure unto him.

Consider those words. John is saying when Christ came to this earth, He brought all of heaven with Him. God didn't put any limits on Christ. He is Lord of all, King of all. Everything is subject to Jesus. There is no end to what He can do or give. There's no end to His spirit, His life, or His love. Jesus came as a man and died as a man, but He will never die again. He lives forevermore. And everyone that believes on Christ shall have eternal life.

The book of John says some didn't receive the witness of John the Baptist; others did. Some people may not receive your witness, and some will. So, don't quit. Don't stop. Don't give up. Keep talking for the Lord. At some point, someone is going to listen to what you have to say, and God will have an effect in that person's life through your testimony.

We receive the witness of men. I hear my wife talking about how God saved her. I hear my friend Tim tell the story of how God saved him out of traditions of men and brought him into the light of His love.

Every one of us has a testimony. People testify to what God has done in their lives, and we believe it.

But John goes on to say the witness God gives is greater. If we receive the witness of men, which we do, why would we not believe the witness of God which is greater? The wonder of it is every one of us has had the Lord witness to our own hearts. We don't have to have anybody tell us anything because the Lord has already told us Himself.

God might witness to you through the prayers of the saints. He might do it by the way we talk to you. I remember as a kid, I wanted to get saved. I was crying and squalling, "Lord, save me, forgive me, wash me in your blood. I'm a sinner, and I need you. I'm going to hell, and I don't want to go to hell, Lord. I want to love you. I want to go to heaven."

And then I knew God saved me. I knew I was clean. Oh, I felt so good. I felt like I just took a bath. I felt so much love in my heart that I wanted to go out and embrace the whole world.

Then I wanted to be filled with the power of the Holy Ghost. A bunch of people gathered around me and started praying. We all prayed the Lord would fill me overflowing with His spirit. I had seen and heard others speak in tongues. I saw their witness, and I wanted what they had. But they prayed for me and nothing happened.

Then one day I was by myself in the church, and I got down on my knees in front by the platform. I started crying out to God, begging Him to let me speak with tongues. There wasn't a bunch of people gathered around with their hands all over me. That was done before, but it wasn't God's time. God was waiting for me to get alone.

Suddenly, tongues started coming out of me. I wasn't trying or making up words. They just flowed, and it was so beautiful. It wasn't very long or loud. But it was real. That's my testimony. That's also the testimony of what happened on the day of Pentecost. The spirit of God came over them, and they began to speak with tongues.

The point is each of us has been given a testimony of Christ. It's given to every one of us because mercy and truth have gone before the Lord. And it's all because of what Christ did at the cross.

The question is, what is your testimony? Do you have something to tell somebody? Is there something real in your life? When people talk with you, do they know by the way you speak and act that Christ has become Lord of your life? Do you have a testimony of life or death? Do you have something good to say or do you always grumble?

The world doesn't need professing Christians who go around grumbling and complaining about life. What they need to see and hear in us is the testimony of the living Savior. They need to see a testimony that life in Christ gives us joy unspeakable and full of glory.

Printed in Great Britain
by Amazon

14452857R00058